creating
# handmade cards
step by step

creating
# handmade cards
### step by step

More than 55 unique personalized greetings cards to make
for every occasion, shown in more than 660 photographs

CHERYL OWEN

LORENZ BOOKS

This edition is published by Lorenz Books,
an imprint of Anness Publishing Ltd,
Blaby Road, Wigston, Leicestershire
LE18 4SE; info@anness.com

www.lorenzbooks.com;
www.annesspublishing.com

If you like the images in this book and would
like to investigate using them for publishing,
promotions or advertising, please visit our
website www.practicalpictures.com
for more information.

Editor: Simona Hill
Designer: Ian Sandom
Photographers: Mark Wood and Paul Bricknell
Production Controller: Helen Wang

Acknowledgements
The publishers would like to thank Lucinda
Ganderton for supplying the projects on pages:
62, 70, 80, 81, 87, 89, 99.

# CONTENTS

# INTRODUCTION

Greetings cards have a wide appeal across many cultures. We send them to mark special occasions such as birthdays or Christmas, to keep in touch, and to express goodwill. In sending these tokens to family and friends we are subscribing to a long tradition. Greetings have been sent in written form for hundreds of years, though originally greetings cards were the preserve of the rich, who commissioned them as elaborate gifts that were expensively produced. It was not until the modernization of printing methods and the ability of printers to reproduce colours accurately and at low cost that the market proliferated with cards for Christmas and Valentine's Day. In recent years cards have been produced for every occasion imaginable, as well as plain pictorial cards,

*Below: A pencil-shaped greetings card with a ribbon attachment can be kept and used as a bookmark.*

*Above: A cute greetings card for a new baby, complete with tiny footprints has a timeless quality*

providing an easy way to communicate with friends. A personal and inexpensive gesture, a greetings card can be kept and treasured, and for this reason the tradition is unlikely to be surpassed by contemporary text messaging or email.

The craft of making greetings cards has grown in popularity, alongside the wider availability of specially designed craft materials, beautiful handmade papers, and the use of the internet for exchanging ideas. As handcrafted cards form a larger part of stationery ranges in gift shops, and are perceived to be of a high value, so the fashion for designing and making them has grown.

Choosing to make and send a greetings card that is handcrafted to suit the style, interests and specific occasion to be celebrated by the recipient

*Above: Decorative motifs are appropriate for use on greetings cards. This one has a folk art quality and has been made in a striking colour scheme.*

makes the gift more personal. It shows how much you care, and the receiver will appreciate the thought and effort that has gone into making the card.

Greetings cards can be quickly made with minimal materials and financial outlay. Because they are quick to make they are an ideal craft for people with busy lives, who will enjoy the pleasure and satisfaction of making a professional-looking card that will be something to treasure.

This beautiful book presents more than 55 unique greetings card ideas for every landmark occasion, such as Christmas, Easter, wedding anniversaries, engagements and the arrival of a new baby, as well as cards to send just to keep in touch. There are projects for beginners as well as for accomplished card makers. All the projects featured are described with concise step-by-step instructions and easy-to-follow photographs. Many are simple enough to make quickly, and in multiples, so are suitable to produce for invitations or for Christmas cards, for example. Or you could lavish time and care to create a one-of-a-kind card for a special person.

A wide range of design styles are presented too, to cater for every taste. There are retro ideas, such as a card for passing a driving test featuring an old black and white photograph, styled with photo corners like an old-fashioned album. Traditional Christmas cards with a festive theme sit alongside contemporary designs. There are cute and colourful cards for baby's birthday, feminine, lacy and embroidered creations for female relatives, as well as garden-themed cards for men.

A comprehensive techniques chapter at the start of the book shows all the basic skills required for the projects, from stencilling images and painting backgrounds, to adding modelled clay motifs and making envelopes for unconventional cards. In addition, templates are provided for every card where needed, so that you can ensure a professional finish is achieved. Once you have mastered new crafts for card making, be inventive and create your own innovative designs.

*Above: Bold buttons can be recycled from the button box to make a quick and stylish card that would be appropriate to send for many occasions, as well as just to keep in touch.*

# Card-making techniques

However original and inspired your designs, they need to be perfectly crafted to make really beautiful, effective greetings cards. This section covers the basic techniques used in the book, from simple card-making to achieving different paint effects, and includes lots of clever tips to give your creations a professional finish. Always read all the instructions for a project before embarking upon it and, if it includes skills that are new to you, experiment on scrap materials first. Follow either the metric or imperial measurements but not a combination of the two.

# EQUIPMENT

For safety and comfort, work on a clean, flat, well-lit surface. Keep all sharp tools and adhesives beyond the reach of children and pets. Clean tools thoroughly after usage.

## Cutting tools

*Always use sharp tools for cutting, and change your knife blades frequently, as blunt blades are liable to tear paper.*

### Knives

Craft knives cut materials neatly and are better than scissors for cutting straight lines, especially on card (stock). Always use a craft knife on a cutting mat, preferably one with a self-healing surface. Cut straight edges with a craft knife against a metal ruler. Retract the knife blade when it is not in use.

Card can be scored with the back of a craft knife blade, but for the best results use a bone folder. This traditional bookbinder's tool will impress the surface of the card but will not cut or weaken it. After making the fold you can also use the bone folder to sharpen the crease by running it flat along the fold.

▼ *Careful measuring and cutting is important: a cutting mat with a printed grid keeps right angles accurate; a clear ruler is useful for positioning lines but you will also need a metal ruler to guide your craft knife.*

### Scissors

Choose scissors that are comfortable to handle. You may find it easier to cut intricate shapes with small, sharp-pointed scissors rather than a craft knife. Cut fabric, ribbon and threads with fabric or embroidery scissors and do not use these on paper or card as they will blunt quickly. Use pinking shears and other decorative-edged scissors to give interesting, shapely edges to your creations.

### Guillotines and die cutters

If you intend to make lots of cards, consider purchasing a guillotine. It should have a measured grid for accurate cutting, and some models will cut decorative edges and rounded corners. Plastic templates and low-level cutters are also available for use with

Synthetic sponge

Cutter

Natural sponge

Cookie cutter

Fancy-edge scissors

▲ *As well as special punches and cutters, standard household equipment such as cookie cutters and pinking shears can be useful in card-making. Small sponges are handy for applying paint.*

die-cutting equipment. Paper punches are available in many different designs and are mainly used to cut out decorative shapes, but the larger sizes can be used to punch out the windows of window cards.

### Punching holes

Use a standard desk double-hole punch to make pairs of holes to thread with ribbon or cord for fastening, or a single hole punch for single holes. A hole punch, which has heads in a number of different sizes arranged on a wheel, is a useful tool for making single holes. To pierce small holes you can use a bradawl, resting on a cutting mat.

### Cutting wire and sheet metal

Use wire snippers to cut wire and round-nosed pliers to manipulate it. Cut sheet metal with metal cutters or an old pair of scissors, bearing in mind that the metal will blunt the blades.

# Drawing, painting and sticking

*As with all crafts, you will get the best results if you always buy the best quality materials you can afford. It is sensible to start with a few basic items and build up your collection gradually.*

## Drawing

Use an HB pencil for drawing. Keep pencils sharpened to a point or use propelling pencils. Draw squares and rectangles using a ruler and set square so that all the lines are straight and the angles accurate. Draw circles with compasses or use a circular stencil for small sizes. Plastic or metal stencils in various shapes are available for drawing around and cutting out. Consider cookie cutters for simple shapes too – they can be good for children's motifs.

▼ *Spray adhesive, glue sticks and PVA (white) glue all stick paper, and glue dots hold small ornaments securely. Double-sided tape is neat and clean, and masking tape is helpful when positioning components.*

Paint palette

▼ *Buy a few good water-colour brushes in a range of sizes, plus a flat-tipped stencil brush. You can buy palettes for mixing paint, but an old white plate is just as good.*

Flat artist's brush

Stencil brush

Fine artist's brush

PVA (white) glue

Glue stick

Glue spreader

Spray adhesive

Glue dots

Clear glue

Round-nosed pliers

Pliers

Double-sided tape

## Applying paint

Paint with good quality artist's paintbrushes and clean the brushes immediately after use. A flat brush, a medium round brush and a fine brush are the most versatile. Stencil with a flat-ended stencil brush. Paint can also be applied with natural or synthetic sponges to create particular effects.

## Adhesives

Read the manufacturers' instructions for all adhesives and test them on scrap materials before use. Work in a well-ventilated room and protect the work surface with scrap paper or newspaper.

Use spray adhesive to stick layers of paper and card together. PVA (white) glue is cheap and very versatile. It will stick paper, card, fabric and wood. All-purpose household glue is strong and will stick many materials, but is best for gluing small pieces as it does not spread evenly over a large surface. Leave items stuck with PVA and all-purpose household glue flat while the glue dries. Paper glue will stick lightweight paper, and is clean and easy to use.

Double-sided tape is a neat way to join paper and card. It is available in a few widths, with 15mm/⅝in being the most versatile. Motifs can be cut from double-sided adhesive sheets and sprinkled with glitter or accent beads (minute beads without holes).

Glue dots, supplied on a backing tape or sheet, stick small items quickly as no drying time is needed. Use adhesive foam pads to raise motifs above a surface, layering them for extra height. They are available in very small sizes but larger pads can be cut to fit. Attach photographs and other pictures with photo mounts at the corners.

Use low-tack masking tape to stick items temporarily, or to mask areas to be painted (but check first that it will not tear the surface when you remove it).

## Using adhesives

Spread glue with a plastic glue spreader or improvise and use a scrap of card. Use a cocktail stick (toothpick) to apply tiny spots of glue. Spray adhesive must be used in a well-ventilated room. Spraying into a large cardboard box stops it drifting on to other surfaces.

# MATERIALS

Apart from the papers that form the foundation of your gift cards, plus suitable adhesives, all the materials you will need are decorative.

# Paper and paint

*A fabulous range of paper and card (stock) is widely available nowadays, and a single sheet of beautiful paper can be enough to make or decorate many cards. Envelopes can be bought ready-made in standard sizes, and you can design your cards to fit these. Alternatively, you can make your own envelopes from matching or co-ordinating paper in any size you choose.*

### Card blanks
Ready-made card blanks are available in a wide range of shapes and styles. They will fit standard-size envelopes and often come with their own envelopes. Window cards and gift tags are also available. Cutting card to make your own greetings cards offers more variety, however, as you can use the material you like and cut it to the exact size required.

### Paper and card
Art shops and specialist paper suppliers stock papers from all over the world. Mass-produced paper and card is available in a vast array of colours, weights and textures and lots of different prices, depending on quality, texture and finish.

Some are coated to give pearlescent, metallic, glittery and even futuristic holographic effects. Tactile embossed and textured papers add interest to a greetings card. Realistic papers resembling fabric, animal skin and wood are lightweight and not as bulky as the real thing. Look for papers incorporating petals, metallic fragments or textural fibres. Mulberry paper is lightweight, but very strong. It is very fibrous and should be torn rather than cut to look most effective.

Papers printed with beautiful patterns or even embroidered need little other embellishment to make stunning greetings cards. These are often sold as gift wrap, so you could make a card that

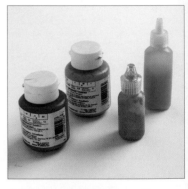

▲ *Water-based paints such as acrylics are ideal for use on paper and card. They are easy and clean to use, fast-drying and available in a vast range of colours. Water-based fabric paints and other special media come in containers with thin nozzles for direct application.*

co-ordinates with the gift wrap. Packs of origami papers and books or packs of patterned papers can be used together to create a theme for your cards, but you can also use scraps of wallpaper to introduce pattern. Many papers are specially packaged in small quantites with co-ordinating colourways or themes for scrapbooking. They are useful for providing small quantities of lots of different types of paper. Copyright-free books offer printed motifs suitable for every occasion. Layer them with translucent and vellum papers to create designs full of depth and interesting colour effects. This technique is especially good for creating nostalgic and "aged" pieces of work.

◀ *Ready-made window cards, with their accompanying envelopes, can be used to frame a photograph or drawing for an instant personalized greeting.*

## Paints

These are used to decorate and transform a plain piece of paper or card with colour and texture. Paint is a versatile medium and can be used to create lots of different effects for background coverage, or to add tiny details as a finishing touch.

Before using any paint, test it on a spare piece of paper or card, as some paints may cause plain paper to warp or soak through to the other side of the sheet. In general, water-based paints are most suitable for use on paper. Acrylic paints, which are water-based, are very versatile: they come in many colours, mix well, dilute, and dry quickly. You can apply thicker paints to the surface of a card and make an impression in the paint with stamps.

Use silk paints to create beautiful effects on silk panels. These water-based paints are applied in areas outlined with outliner (gutta) on silk stretched in an embroidery frame. Large areas need to be coloured quickly before the paint starts to dry, otherwise watermarks will result. Different effects can also be achieved by adding salt crystals to the drying paint.

Relief paints and glitter paints are fun to use. They come in plastic tubes and are applied straight to the surface through a thin nozzle. Try these first on spare paper to ensure that you can

achieve a smooth, continuous line of paint with a professional finish. Masking fluid has a similar consistency to paint. Use it to mask areas that should remain unpainted. Allow the fluid to dry before applying paint to the surface. Once the design has been painted over, and the paint has dried, the dried mask is rubbed away.

Frosting spray gives an etched glass effect. Use it on acetate, masking off a design with sticky-backed plastic.

## Rubber stamping

Ready-made rubber stamps are made to suit every imaginable theme, and enable cards to be produced quickly and with a highly professional finish. They are available as "mounted" designs, meaning they are attached to a block of wood, or "unmounted" so that you can apply them to clear plastic, which helps accurate positioning of the motif. You can also make your own simple stamps from Neoprene foam. Stamp designs on to the greetings card using an ink pad and enhance the image with

▲ *Plain, printed and textured papers of every description are available from art, craft and stationery suppliers. While some handmade and decorative papers can be expensive, a single sheet can be used to make a number of original cards, and offcuts can be saved for future use.*

embossing powder, before the paint dries, if you wish. Watercolour stamp paints give the appearance of hand-painted images. Rubber stamps can also be used to impress polymer clay before hardening.

▼ *Rubber stamps are easy to use and can be used with inks or paint. You can also apply embossing powder to produce a raised motif.*

Paint

Rubber stamps

Embossing powder

Ink pad

# Embellishments

*Greetings cards can be decorated with all kinds of unexpected materials. The main limitation is that they should not be too heavy, or they will tip the card over. Many companies now manufacture "card toppers", which are pre-formed decorations that need only glue dots to hold them in place. However, making your own is far more satisfying.*

### Fabric and haberdashery

If you are a keen needleworker, you will undoubtedly already have a stash of fabric and ribbon offcuts, ornamental buttons, embroidery threads (floss), beads and sequins. These are all ideal for decorating greetings cards and can be stuck in position using PVA (white) glue. A tiny panel of embroidery or appliqué is quick and easy to sew but can have a lot of impact as a feature of a greetings card. Small panels of silk or other fabrics can also be decorated with fabric paints.

Backing fabric with medium-weight iron-on interfacing stops it fraying and makes it easier to handle and cut out.

### Natural materials

Look to the natural world for materials to decorate your cards. Small pieces of driftwood and balsa wood may be light enough to use. Feathers have a natural resilience that will allow them to be folded into a card without being crushed, and they will add a delicate look to your creations.

Collect fallen leaves and twigs or pick flowers to press in a flower press or between the pages of a heavy book. Specialist shops sell seashells to underline a nautical theme.

### Moulded decorations

Polymer clay is available in lots of colours, as well as metallic and other special finishes. The colours can also be blended to create new shades or partly blended for a marbled effect. Bake the clay in an oven to harden it, following the manufacturer's instructions. Neoprene foam is also very useful for three-dimensional decorations. It is soft and pliable and should be glued in position with all-purpose household glue.

Relief paint

Buttons and toggles

Embroidered motifs

▲ *Relief paints can be applied straight from the container to make simple raised designs. All kinds of buttons and embroidered motifs also add three-dimensional interest, but need to be very securely attached.*

▼ *Tiny ornaments, glitter, sprinkles and wire add lustre to card designs. Embellish them further with decorative fastenings and finish by tying the layers together with pretty ribbon or cord.*

Polymer clay

Lurex cord

Embroidery thread (floss)

Wire

Ribbon

Glitter

Sequins

Metal plaques

Eyelets

Snap fasteners

Brads

Photo corners

## Metallics

Apply fine metallic leaf over a coat of gold size to create luxurious gilded greetings cards. For the finest effects you can use tiny amounts of real gold and silver leaf, but a cheaper option is Dutch metal leaf, which is available in gold, silver, copper and other colours. Alternatively, you can rub metallic wax on embossed paper and clay surfaces to highlight the raised areas.

You can also enhance your designs using fine metal sheet, embossed with simple images. Aluminium, brass and copper foils of suitable thickness for embossing are available from craft suppliers. Wire is another option for adding the gleam of metal to cards, and is easy to shape into coils, frames and motifs. Fine wire is available in different thicknesses and colours from craft stores and jewellery-making suppliers.

## Stickers and glitter

Create a greetings card instantly by sticking on a row of ready-made stickers. There are stickers for every occasion, made of card, plastic, fabric or even diamanté jewellery stones. All have an adhesive backing so they are ready for use. There are also ready-made three-dimensional motifs to attach to make an instant greetings card, but you can give any sticker or cut-out an extra dimension by attaching it to a foam pad. Consider, too, charms, embroidered patches and woven or printed labels. Save broken or unwanted costume jewellery, such as odd earrings, and

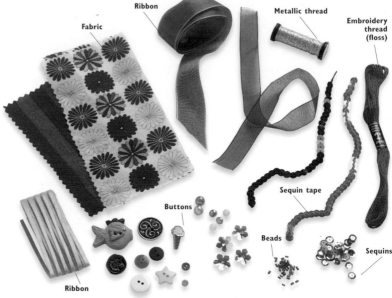

Fabric · Ribbon · Metallic thread · Embroidery thread (floss) · Buttons · Sequin tape · Beads · Sequins · Ribbon

dismantle it so that you can use the individual elements as hanging ornaments on the front of cards.

Card decorations can be further embellished with tiny elements such as glitter, accent beads and sequin dust (the tiny holes punched from sequins). "Sprinkles" are tiny plastic shapes like miniature sequins but without holes. Use them in the same way as sequin dust, pouring them over a coat of glue then shaking off the excess.

▲ *Haberdashery stores provide rich pickings for greetings card decoration, from scraps of pretty fabrics to novelty buttons, ribbons, sequins and embroidery threads, which are all light in weight and easy to attach to card.*

## Fastenings

As an alternative to gluing layers together invisibly, you can turn mounts and fastenings into decorative features by using items such as brads, snap fasteners, and eyelets. Snap fasteners, available from craft suppliers, resemble those used for dressmaking but have attractive tops. Brads, similar to regular stationery paper fasteners, are available in many styles and finishes. Eyelets give a utilitarian look to a greetings card: they are applied with eyelet pliers or an eyelet tool and a tack hammer.

You can also lace or tie layers together using lengths of ribbon, thonging, cord, paper, hemp string or raffia. Ribbon is available in numerous widths and textures. Wire-edged ribbon will hold its shape when tied in a bow.

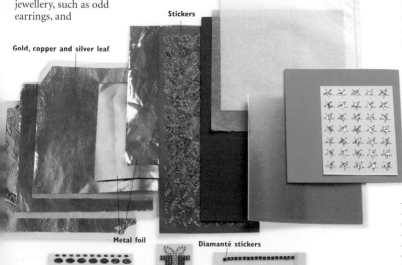

Gold, copper and silver leaf · Stickers · Metal foil · Diamanté stickers

◀ *Sparkling touches of metallic leaf or embossed foil can be used to enhance your own designs, but you can also create effective cards using ready-made motifs in foil, glitter or tiny gems. For more subtle effects, add contrasts of texture in the form of vellum, tissue or interesting handmade papers.*

# WORKING WITH PAPER

Paper and card (stock) come in many different weights and qualities, so it is wise to experiment with the basic techniques to check that your chosen material will produce the effect you want.

# Papercraft techniques

*Most paper is easy to fold and cut, especially if it is lightweight, but you need to aim for accuracy in all these basic tasks to achieve satisfying, professional-looking results.*

## CUTTING

For best results, cut straight lines using a craft knife against a metal ruler rather than a pair of scissors. Always take care when handling blades.

**1** Rest the sheet on a cutting mat and cut straight lines using a craft knife, guiding the blade along a metal ruler. When cutting card (card stock), do not press very hard or attempt to cut right through with the first pass, but gradually cut deeper and deeper.

**2** You may find it easier to cut intricately shaped motifs or small circles with a small pair of sharp-pointed scissors. Hold the scissors in one position and turn the paper in the other hand, rather than trying to move the scissors round the shape.

## FOLDING

Make sure the edges are perfectly aligned before creasing the fold.

When folding card, score it first, then fold along the scored line. Press the flat of a bone folder on the fold and run it smoothly along its length. If you do not have a bone folder, run your thumb along the fold to flatten it.

## SCORING

Although paper can be folded simply by aligning the edges and flattening the fold, scoring the surface of card first gives a neater, sharper finish.

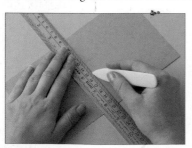

**1** A bone folder is recommended for scoring as it will indent a line to fold along without breaking the surface of the card. The right or wrong side of the card can be scored. Lay it on a firm surface and score along the fold line with the pointed end of the folder resting against a ruler.

**2** Alternatively, lightly score the card with the back of a craft knife blade, taking care to break the top surface only and not to cut right through the card.

## USING SPRAY ADHESIVE

The room must be well ventilated when you are using spray adhesive.

Protect the surrounding area with scrap paper or newspaper, or place the card inside a large cardboard box. If sticking large sheets, smooth them outwards from the centre to avoid creases and air bubbles.

# STICKING MOTIFS

Motifs cut from card and other materials can be made to stand proud of the card front by mounting them on adhesive foam pads or glue dots.

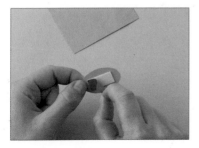

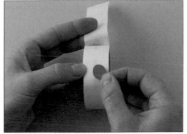

**1** Select a foam pad that is smaller than the motif, or cut an appropriate shape from a large pad. Stick it to the back of the motif, positioning it centrally. Peel off the backing paper then press the motif in position.

**2** Press a glue dot on its backing paper to the back of a motif, positioning it centrally. Peel away the backing paper leaving the glue dot in place, then press the motif in position on the card.

# STRENGTHENING PAPER

Mounting paper on a sheet of card makes it sturdy enough to use for the main body of a greetings card.

**1** Cut the paper 1cm/⅜in larger all round than the required size. Apply spray adhesive to the back of the paper then stick it to a sheet of card.

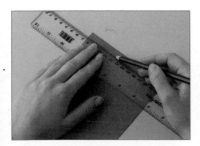

**2** Turn the card over and draw the size required for the greetings card. Resting on a cutting mat, cut out the card and paper together using a craft knife and metal ruler.

## USING VELLUM

Translucent vellum paper can be used to overlay patterns or pictures to create subtle colour effects.

Change the colour of vellum by applying it to card of a contrasting or deeper colour. Here, light blue is applied to pink card to create lilac. Attach vellum with spray adhesive or "invisible" glue dots.

▲ *Here, a glittery striped paper has been applied to pink card. A wooden decoration is tied to the front with cord.*

# Tearing paper

*Softly torn paper edges can add extra interest to a greetings card, especially if you are using a fibrous material such as mulberry paper. Torn edges usually look best when contrasted with the sharp, neatly cut edges of other elements in the design. The overall effect of torn edges is quite feminine.*

## CREATING A TORN EDGE AGAINST A RULER

Tearing paper against a ruler controls the tear, so that the edge is attractively torn but straight. This is particularly useful if you are using a handmade paper that has a deckle edge but needs two sides of the paper to be torn to make the overall size smaller. Tearing the third and fourth edges to size will match the deckle edges. For stronger paper dampen the tear line first to weaken the fibres.

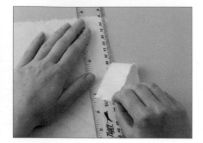

**1** Hold a ruler firmly on the paper where you wish to tear it. Tear the paper against the ruler. If you are using a printed paper with a white core, this will appear uppermost along the edge: to avoid it tear with the printed side down.

**2** If the paper is too thick or strong to tear easily, run a moistened artist's brush along the intended tear line first to soften and weaken the fibres. Allow the paper to absorb the water for a few moments then tear it against a ruler as before.

**3** For a freer effect you can simply tear the paper between your fingers. If you follow the grain of the paper the torn edge will still be relatively straight.

## CREATING A TORN-EDGE MOTIF

Simple collages and other applied paper designs in a naive style can be enhanced by tearing rather than cutting out the motifs. This method suits pictures of natural, curved forms such as leaves and flowers.

**1** Draw the motif on the back of the paper, leaving a margin of at least 5mm/¼in around the motif. Tear along the drawn line by holding the motif between the thumb and fingers of one hand close to the drawn line and pulling the paper around the image toward you with the other hand. Tear slowly and carefully and, for accuracy, gradually move the fingers holding the paper along the line.

▲ *The torn flower motif on this colourful card has the naive quality of folk art.*

### POSITIONING MOTIFS

To judge the position of one or more motifs, hold the traced template over the front of the card or attach it lightly at the top using masking tape.

Slip the motifs under the tracing, adjusting them as necessary until they match the template. Remove the tracing carefully when all the motifs are securely in place.

# Working with templates

*All the templates you will need in order to make the greetings cards in this book can be found together in a section at the end. You will need to trace or photocopy them and scale them up or down as necessary before use.*

## TRANSFERRING TEMPLATES

If you need to use the template only once it may be sufficient simply to transfer your tracing. If a template is to be used repeatedly, it is worth cutting it out of stiff card (card stock), which you can then draw round.

I Trace the template on to tracing paper. Redraw it on the wrong side using a soft pencil. Tape the tracing right side up on paper or card with masking tape. Redraw the design with a sharp pencil to transfer it.

2 Transfer the template to a piece of card if you intend to use it more than a few times. Cut out the card template, which can then be drawn around many times.

## ENLARGING AND REDUCING TEMPLATES ON A GRID

If you don't have access to a photocopier you can rescale a template by redrawing it on a smaller or larger grid.

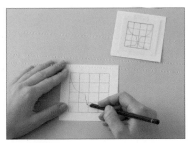

I To enlarge or reduce a motif on a grid, tape a piece of tracing paper over the original design with masking tape. Draw a square or rectangle on top, enclosing the image, and divide it up with rows of vertical and horizontal lines, making equal-sized squares or rectangles. Draw a square or rectangle of the required finished size to the same proportions as the shape on the tracing paper. Divide it with the same number of vertical and horizontal lines.

2 Redraw the image, working on one square or rectangle at a time.

3 Look at the new design as a whole and redraw any areas that do not seem to match up or to "flow" well.

## ENLARGING AND REDUCING ON A PHOTOCOPIER

It is sometimes necessary to enlarge or reduce a motif. For accuracy and speed, use a photocopier to do this.

I Decide what width you want the final motif to be. Next, measure the width of the original motif you intend to photocopy in millimetres. Divide the first measurement by the second and multiply the result by 100 to find the percentage by which to enlarge the motif. For example, a motif needs to be enlarged to 50mm and the original width is 40mm (50 divided by 40 = 1.25, and 1.25 x 100 = 125). Therefore, the motif must be photocopied at 125 per cent. Remember that an enlargement will be more than 100 per cent and a reduction less than 100 per cent.

## USING READY-MADE TEMPLATES

Lots of ready-made plastic or metal templates of useful motifs are available to draw round. Clear plastic makes it easy to position the template correctly.

I A number of motifs of different shapes or sizes are often available on a single sheet. A circle template is particularly useful.

# Window cards

*It is easy to make window cards to your exact requirements. They can be cut to any shape. If you plan to make a series of cards, use a large paper punch to punch matching windows. If you have embroidered a card front, or attached motifs with brads, or sewn a motif in place with wire, the underside of the card front can be covered with a facing, which will hide any fixings.*

▼ *These ready-made window cards have metallic paper behind the windows and display a decorative leaf and a fabulous metal elephant.*

## MAKING A TRIPLE-SECTION WINDOW CARD

For neatness, a window card is usually constructed in three sections: two of the three sections form the card front and back, and the last section is a facing that is next to the front but 5mm/¼in narrower than it. The facing is stuck to the underside of the front to hide the raw edges of whatever is shown in the window and the backs of any fixings. The piece of card is folded into three sections with the left-hand section being the facing that is slightly narrower than the card front and back.

**1** Draw the dimensions of the card on the wrong side of a piece of card (stock). For example, if you want your folded card to measure 18cm/7in high x 10cm/4in wide, you need to draw a rectangle measuring 29.5 x 18cm/11¾ x 7in. Cut out the rectangle using a craft knife and metal ruler and working on a cutting mat.

**2** Still working on the wrong side of the card, score and fold it 9.5cm/3¾in from the left-hand short edge and 10cm/4in from the right-hand short edge, keeping the folds parallel with the short edges. Open the card out flat again.

**3** Draw the window on the wrong side of the middle section, positioning it centrally between the folds. Cut out the window with a craft knife, resting on a cutting mat.

▶ *This pretty card has strings of sequins behind the window. Three additional sequins are stuck to the card front using glue dots.*

**4** Cut the motif, or the background paper or card that will go behind the motif in the window, making it approximately 1cm/⅜in larger all round than the window. Apply 5mm/¼in-wide double-sided tape all round the window on the wrong side.

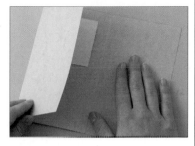

**5** Peel off the backing strips and stick the motif behind the window. Apply 5mm/¼in-wide double-sided tape to the cut edges of the facing section. Peel off the backing strips and stick the facing section to the underside of the front.

# Working with inserts

*A greetings card with an insert, or inner sheet, always looks very classy. The insert is also practical as it hides any fixings inside the card front, and a pale insert inside a dark-coloured or heavily textured card provides a good surface on which to write your greeting legibly.*

## MAKING AN UNFOLDED INSERT

If you are making a card with a separate front and back bound together, the insert can also be made from one or two loose sheets of paper.

**1** Cut one or two sheets of lightweight paper 5mm/¼in smaller on all sides than the front and back of the card.

**2** Arrange the insert on the card back, matching the left edges of the sheets. Place the front on top.

**3** Join the layers along the left edge in your chosen style, using brads or eyelets.

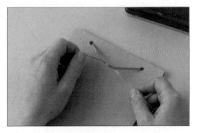

**4** Alternatively, punch a pair of holes in the left edge and tie with ribbon.

## MAKING A FOLDED INSERT

In a standard folded card, a paper insert is simply folded to match and glued near the fold so that it opens with the card.

**1** Cut the insert 5mm/¼in smaller on all sides than the card. Fold the insert in half and run a line of paper glue along the fold.

**2** Stick the insert inside the card, matching the fold lines and making sure the border is even at the top and bottom.

# Punching holes

*It's often necessary to punch holes when making cards and gift tags, either for decoration, such as when you want a contrasting colour to show through the holes, or for practical purposes, such as to sew or thread ribbon through. Make sure the holes you make will be large enough for practical applications before you begin, and for a more professional finish, ensure that they are lined up correctly by marking their position with a pencil and ruler.*

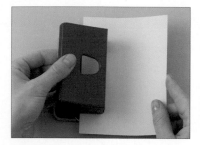

**1** Punch holes for inserting ribbon or cord fastenings with a single or double hole punch. The holes made by a standard desk hole punch will be 5mm/¼in in diameter.

**2** A single hole punch usually has heads of different sizes that screw into the handle. Resting on a cutting mat, hold the hole punch upright on the card and hit the end with a tack hammer to punch the hole.

**3** Alternatively, rest the card on a cutting mat and twist the hole punch to cut the hole. This works well with new punches and on paper rather than card (stock), but will be less effective as the punch blunts.

◄ **4** Use a shaped paper punch to create decoratively shaped holes.

► **5** Don't discard the punched shapes, as they can also be used to embellish greetings cards. Stick each one in place with a glue dot or adhesive foam pad. If the shapes are very small or intricate, such as these sprigs, use the smallest size glue dots, which are usually supplied on a sheet.

◄ *This bright card uses decorative punched holes to great effect. Leaf sprigs are punched in a band of turquoise paper and the punched shapes are then applied with glue dots. A strip of turquoise paper cut using decorative-edged scissors and punched with a 2mm/¹⁄₁₆in hole punch is used as a border on the contrasting lime green card. The remaining punched shapes can be slipped inside the card as confetti.*

# USING BRADS

Attach motifs or fasten the front and back of cards together with brads. Numerous decorative styles are available, and they are simple to use and very versatile as they can be opened to remove or add items.

**I** Resting the card on a cutting mat, pierce small holes through the pieces to be joined using a bradawl.

**2** Insert the brads through the holes.

**3** Splay open the prongs on the underside of the card.

# USING SNAP FASTENINGS

Join layers together with craft snap fasteners. They are the same as dressmaking fasteners but have decorative tops.

**I** Press the pointed end of the top section of the snap fastener through the card layers. If the layers are too thick to do this make a hole with a bradawl before inserting the snap fastener.

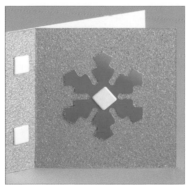

▲ This frosty Christmas card has a punched snowflake attached with a snap fastener. The front of the card is joined to the back with snap fasteners too.

# APPLYING EYELETS

Eyelets can be used for the same purposes as brads, except that once they are fixed, they cannot be removed. They can, however, have ribbons or hanging charms threaded through them.

**I** Make a hole for the eyelet with a bradawl or a hole punch. Insert the eyelet into the hole.

**2** Position the eyelet into the recess of a pair of eyelet pliers. Squeeze the handles of the pliers to flatten the eyelet.

**3** Alternatively, use an eyelet tool kit, following the manufacturer's instructions.

# Making envelopes

*Many of the cards you make will fit ready-made standard envelopes, and plastic templates are available to draw around and cut out to make envelopes in your own choice of paper. However, it is easy to make your own envelopes when you need them for cards in unusual sizes. It is also worth making your own template if you find a size that suits your purposes.*

## BASIC ENVELOPE

You can adapt this basic design to make square or long envelopes.

▶ *A plain envelope is easy to make in any size or shape, and can be tailored to match and co-ordinate with your cards.*

**1** Draw the size of the card front on scrap paper, adding 5mm/¼in to each edge. Draw the flap at the upper edge half the depth of the front. Draw the back at the lower edge, reducing the depth by 2cm/¾in.

**2** Draw a tab 2.5cm/1in wide at each side of the front. Draw a curve at each corner, using a circle stencil or drawing around the side of a coin so that all the curves are the same shape. Cut out the template.

**3** Draw round the template on your chosen paper and cut out the envelope. Fold in the side tabs, back and flap along the edges of the front. Open the back and flap out flat again.

**4** Apply 5mm/¼in-wide double-sided tape along the side edges of the back, starting below the curves.

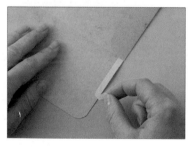

**5** Peel off the backing strips and stick the back over the tabs.

**6** To fasten, tuck the flap inside the back or seal with double-sided tape. Alternatively, seal the flap with a sticker.

◀ *If you prefer, trim the flap of the envelope with decorative-edged scissors, or cut it to a point, trimming the tip in a curve.*

## CUTWORK DESIGN

Stamp your personal style on the envelope as well as its contents by adding a punched or cutwork decoration before making it up.

▼ *A cascade of punched holes appears to flow across the front of this envelope.*

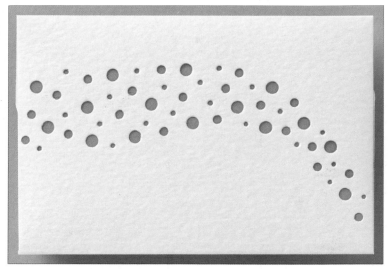

1 Open out the envelope and rest it on a cutting mat. Cut a design or punch decorative holes across the front, working from the right side. For the best result, the card that goes inside should be of a contrasting or different shade.

## MAKING A CLASSIC WALLET

This simple envelope has no flap and can be fastened in various ways. Its plain design is ideal when you want to use a beautiful printed paper.

▼ *This classic wallet has holes punched at the top and is tied with ribbon. In sumptuous gold and cream paper it makes a lovely container for a wedding card or gift.*

1 To make a template, measure the card front and draw it on scrap paper, adding 2cm/¾in to the side edges and 5mm/¼in to the top and bottom edges. Draw the back at the lower edge the same size as the front. Draw a tab at each side of the front 1.5cm/⅝in wide. Draw a curve at each end of the tab. Cut out the wallet template.

2 Cut the envelope out of paper. Fold in the tabs and back along the front edges, then open the back out flat. Apply 5mm/¼in-wide double-sided tape to the side edges of the back, stopping 5mm/¼in from the top and bottom. Peel off the backing strips and stick over the tabs.

# MAKING A PADDED ENVELOPE

Present a delicate greetings card in a padded envelope for protection.

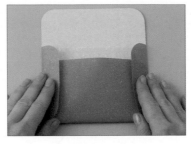

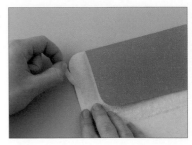

**I** Draw the dimensions of the card front on scrap paper, adding 1cm/⅜in to each edge, and make a template as for the Basic Envelope. Cut bubble wrap to fit the front and back sections and glue inside the envelope, with the smooth side uppermost.

**2** Fold in the back then fold the side tabs over. Open the tabs out flat again.

**3** Apply 5mm/¼in-wide double-sided tape along the outer edges of the tabs, starting 2cm/¾in from the upper edges. Peel off the backing strips and stick the tabs over the back. Seal the envelope by sticking the flap over the back with double-sided tape.

# MAKING A CARD-BACKED ENVELOPE

To prevent a greetings card being bent or folded in the mail, send it in a stiffened envelope.

**I** Measure the card front and draw it on scrap paper, adding 5mm/¼in to each edge. Draw the flap at the upper edge half the depth of the front. Draw 2.5cm/1in-wide tabs on the other three sides of the front.

**2** Draw a curve at each corner using a template or coin. Cut out the template and use it to cut the envelope from paper. Fold the envelope along the edges of the front then open all the sides out flat again.

**3** Apply 5mm/¼in-wide double-sided tape along the outer edges of the tabs, between the curves.

**4** Cut the back from stiff card (stock) the same size as the front, then trim 1cm/⅜in from the top and 3mm/⅛in from one side. Place the card back on the front.

**5** With the lower edges matching, peel off the backing strips and stick the side tabs, then the lower tab, over the back.

**6** To fasten, seal the flap to the back with double-sided tape. Alternatively, seal the flap with a sticker.

# MAKING A LINED ENVELOPE

A lining in a matching or contrasting colour gives a touch of luxury to an envelope. Choose lightweight paper so it is not too bulky.

I Cut out the basic envelope. Cut the front and flap from the lining paper, trimming 3mm/⅛in from the outer edges. Stick the lining to the inside of the envelope using spray adhesive.

2 Continue making up the envelope. For best results, seal the envelope by tucking the flap into the back.

▲ *An elegant tissue lining enhances the appearance of the envelope as well as giving greater protection to the contents.*

# NOVELTY ENVELOPE

Create an amusing envelope for a child in a special shape. Your design must have an opening large enough to slip the card into. Alternatively make an attractive envelope to hold a small gift.

I Cut a pair of elephants from paper. Resting on scrap paper, apply paper glue along the edges on the back of one elephant, leaving the straightest edge open.

2 Stick the elephants together. Stick on card ears and joggle eyes. Punch matching holes at the top to fasten with ribbon.

▲ *The elephant template at the back of the book is used to make this funny envelope to contain a tiny card. Enlarge the template as necessary for a larger card. A joggle eye and*

*a scythe-shaped sequin for a tusk are stuck in place using glue dots. Curling gift-wrap ribbon is tied through punched holes to fasten the envelope.*

# MAKING A BOX ENVELOPE

For a three-dimensional greetings card you may need to custom-make a box especially to fit it. These are quick and easy to make. For added protection for the card, you can line the box and lid with bubble wrap, fill the box with shredded tissue, or wrap the card in tissue paper.

**1** To make a template, measure the card front and draw it on scrap paper, adding 5mm/¼in to each edge. This will be the base. Lay the card flat on its back and measure its depth. Draw a side to the box along each edge that is the depth of the card plus 3mm/⅛in.

**2** Add a tab 1.5cm/⅝in wide to each end of two opposite box sides, drawing a slanted side to each tab from the corner of the box base. Cut out the template and use it to cut the box from card (stock), using a craft knife and metal ruler and working on a cutting mat.

**3** Score along the lines using a bone folder and fold up the sides of the box. Stick the tabs inside the ends of the adjacent sides using double-sided tape. Make a lid in the same way as the box, adding 2mm/⅛in to each edge of the lid top so that it fits over the sides of the box.

# QUICK WALLETS

The sides of a simple wallet can be fastened decoratively with brads or eyelets. Cut the wallet wide enough to allow for the side fastenings as well as taking the greetings card.

**1** Fold a sheet of paper in half and punch a row of holes along the sides.

**2** Starting at the lower edge, oversew each side with paper string. Work back to the lower edge and tie the ends together.

▲ *The top of this handmade paper wallet fastens with paper string tied around circles of paper attached to the front and back using eyelets – this should be done with the paper opened out flat, before the side edges are stitched together. The holes along the side edges are punched 2cm/¾in apart and threaded with paper string.*

## NOW TRY THIS

▲ The sides of a quick wallet can be joined using various stitches. In this back-stitch version using a double length of silver embroidery thread (floss), a shell-shaped sequin and a small bead are threaded on to each stitch on the wallet

front. The wallet is made of Neoprene foam, which is very quick and easy to cut and sew, and it is sealed with a length of ribbon wrapped around the centre and tied with another length of silver thread trimmed with more sequins and a larger

▲ This handmade paper wallet has bands of beaded trim glued along the side edges. It is fastened with ribbons glued in the centre of the top edges. Flower sequins conceal the join and trim the ends of the ribbon.

# MAKING QUICK ENVELOPES

The simplest envelopes can be made with a few folds and no side flaps.

▼ *Toile de jouy wallpaper is used for this quick envelope. The flap is edged with glitter paint to emphasize its curvaceous shape.*

I Make an instant envelope with a flap by folding a rectangle of paper into thirds. The sheet should be 2cm/¾in wider than the height of the front of the greetings card and three times the width of the front plus 3cm/1¼in. Open it out flat again and stick the front to the back with 5mm/¼in-wide double-sided tape at each side. Cut the flap edge in a decorative shape if you wish.

◀ 2 Alternatively, for a square greetings card, mark the centre of the side edges of a square of paper with a pencil. The paper should be half as long again as each edge. For example, for a 14cm/5½in square card, cut a 21cm/8¼in square of paper. Fold the paper diagonally between the pencil marks so that the corners meet at the centre.

▶ 3 Place the greetings card inside the envelope, close the flaps and seal the envelope with a decorative motif or a sticker at the centre.

# DESIGN THEMES FOR CARDS

Your original designs for cards will be unique to you: if you wish you can tailor each one to suit the recipient, but your own taste is likely to influence the style of most of your creations. Clarifying the themes you wish to follow can be helpful as you build up stocks of paper and decorative materials.

## Contemporary style

*Greetings cards immediately look up-to-date when made with modern materials. Acetate and plain translucent papers have a contemporary look, and superbly realistic papers resembling distressed metals are also appealing. Experiment with shiny materials on a matt background of the same colour for an understated look. Make envelopes and wallets of Neoprene foam or acetate fastened with plastic thonging for a funky way to present cards or gifts.*

Natural motifs with distinctive outlines are very popular now and are best when used boldly. Even antique-style motifs can be given a modern twist, maybe by enlarging just a section of the design. Update traditional designs by working them in unexpected materials – such as stencilling with metallic paint on paper incorporating metallic fragments. Spray acetate with frosting spray for an etched glass effect. Clever laser-cut designs occur throughout contemporary interior design, and the style also suits greetings cards, using cutwork motifs in stylish papers.

Glamour plays an unashamed part in modern style. Wrap a gift in pearlized paper and bind it with a length of diamanté trim. Add gemstone stickers or sprinkle loose glitter or accent beads on shapes such as a candelabra or high heeled shoes cut from a double-sided adhesive sheet.

Alternatively, use sugar paper in subdued colourways, graph paper or lined writing paper for a utilitarian look. Type a message in a simple font then cut the wording into strips and use as tape to bind a present. Punch out a name on a metal tag to tie on a gift or attach it to a greetings card using a chrome brad or eyelet.

### Going digital

The computer, an essential tool in modern life, can be used to create entire cards or just background papers on which to apply decorations. Digital photography offers many creative possibilities, and if you are a keen photographer you will have a wealth of images to choose from. Changing the background colour of an image is a useful manipulation technique, and distracting background details can also be removed. Image-editing software is sophisticated and can produce extraordinary effects.

◀ *For an understated modern Easter card (below left), a repeat design of egg shapes cut from plain and lined translucent paper is arranged on lime green pearlized paper. A traditional flock wallpaper design is given a modern twist (above right) by enlarging it and cutting it from double-sided adhesive sheet, which is then applied to copper-effect card (stock) and sprinkled with copper glitter.*

# Vintage style

*There are many occasions when a vintage-style greetings card fits the bill. These unashamedly romantic creations make perfect Valentine cards and are also ideal for weddings and engagements. To make this style work well you need to develop a magpie's talent for hoarding a multitude of small treasures for possible future use: printed scraps and engraved images, tickets, tags and other ephemera, old letters, fragments of lace or frail patterned silks, ribbons, buttons and bows. All these disparate elements are held in harmony by their soft textures and faded colours, allowing them to be combined in beautiful designs of tremendous richness and depth.*

Traditional materials such as handmade paper and natural fabrics have soft textures and colours to match with vintage embellishments. Marbled papers also suit cards with a vintage theme. And not everything you use needs to be old: there are clever ways to create the look. You can scan or photocopy old letters, or samples of copperplate handwriting, and age your photocopies by painting them with a weak solution of tea. Sprinkle a few instant coffee granules sparingly on the surface before the tea dries. You can buy books of papers printed with vintage handwriting or music scripts to use as backgrounds and borders, and reproductions of 19th-century colour-printed paper scraps. Cotton lace will also age realistically if dyed in a cup of strong, cold tea for a few hours. Rinse in water and spread out to dry naturally.

Sort through old family photographs for useful images. Don't use the originals but photocopy or scan them then age them digitally with a sepia tone, or add a little delicate hand tinting. Frame them with borders of lace or ribbon.

## Vintage embellishments

There are lots of antique-style accessories available to create heritage greetings cards, but you may already have suitable items. Old sewing accessories are ideal: mother-of-pearl buttons are particularly pretty. Small fragments of lace and pieces of embroidery can be framed in a window card. Hang tiny charms and lockets on a luggage label.

Pressed flowers are perfect embellishments for vintage cards, with their soft, faded colours and timeless charm.

Apply a mass of dainty pressed forget-me-nots in a heart shape or linked rings for an engagement card.

Paper doilies are cheap and easily available, but pieces used sparingly as backgrounds can lend vintage designs the look of old cut-paper greetings cards. Books of copyright-free images are another useful resource: photocopies of old engravings stuck to cards make instant greetings cards or sets of invitations or notelets.

Make vintage-style envelopes and wrappings too. Tie up your parcels with string, seal them with sealing wax and decorate them with old stamps or tickets and labels from foreign holidays.

▶ *Scraps of old textiles, manuscripts and printed ephemera are staple ingredients of vintage style. An exquisite scrap of a beaded and embroidered panel is mounted on a background of dark marbled paper (left), while the border of fine lace has a piece of broken jewellery sewn to it. Another eclectic assembly (right) features a pair of distressed luggage labels decorated with a lace fragment and postage stamp and bound with silk ribbon. They are stuck to a section of an old map, tinted with tea and mounted on handmade paper. The strings of the labels are cleverly used to fasten the pages together.*

# Retro style

*The bold designs of the not-so-distant past are now being rediscovered and reinterpreted by modern designers, and the best of them retain their freshness while also evoking fond memories of the 1950s, '60s and '70s. Be inspired by these graphic patterns and images and create witty, retro cards that chime perfectly with today's style.*

Stereotypical images from 1950s advertising, books and periodicals, portraying manly men, domesticated women, perfect children and streamlined homes, are perfect for funny, ironic cards, especially when you want to send an irreverent greeting to a friend: just add your own pithy caption or personalized speech bubbles. Hunt through your older relatives' bookshelves and attics for suitable images, or try second-hand book stores, postcard dealers and charity shops.

Stylized organic motifs dominated 1950s graphic design, and relief paints are ideal for work in this style. The kidney shape was a popular outline and was used for all kinds of items, from the tops of coffee tables to textile motifs. Try stamping the shape with a handmade Neoprene foam stamp on plain paper for retro-style gift wrap. A grey, red and black colour scheme would work well.

Images of basic everyday utensils such as kitchenware were also popular in wallpaper and printed textile designs of the time.

Many of the printed papers available from craft stores for scrapbooking feature retro images of this kind, and they can be used as background designs or cut up as sources of decorative motifs.

### The 1960s

The confident wild designs of the 1960s are easy to reproduce. After the previous decade's insistence on modernism, 1960s designers revived Victorian and Edwardian styles, but with a contemporary twist. This was also the age of op art and psychedelia. Keep the colours bold and vibrant: orange was particularly popular, often combined with sizzling pink or purple. Cut bulbous shapes such as stylized flowers from brightly coloured towelling and cotton fabrics. Chunky plastic buttons and coloured synthetic lace flowers are great for appliqué effects. Cut out curvaceous letters and numbers from suitably patterned papers to add to cards and tags.

### The 1970s

For true 1970s glam-rock style, create a glittery frame for a photograph on the front of a greetings card. Using spray adhesive stick gift wrap or wallpaper with a loud repeat pattern to a card as a background, then top with a slinky silhouette of a dancer cut from glossy sticky-backed plastic. Photocopy or scan a computer image from comics of the time.

Cut stylish Scandinavian furniture shapes from realistic wood veneer paper and apply to a greetings card covered with a scrap of suitable wallpaper to make a quirky card for friends with an interest in interior design. If you can crochet, work a square medallion to adorn the top of a square gift box for a touch of 1970s folksiness.

To complete the retro effect, type your messages and captions in decorative fonts that evoke the period that inspires you.

◀ *This gift box (right) is decorated with simple retro motifs reminiscent of 1950s designs inspired by the dawning space age. Circles are cut freehand from red paper and stuck at random to the box lid, then decorated with smoky blue and black relief paints. On the card (left) a vibrant pop art flower has petals applied in layers cut from orange and grey card and applied to a circle of grey. The background is orange polka-dot gift wrap applied to grey card.*

# Natural style

*Nature provides lots of beautiful materials for card making. Gather feathers, seed pods and twigs when you are out for walks in the countryside, or pick flowers and leaves from the garden to press for future greetings card projects. Pressed ivy and bay leaves are sturdy enough to be painted or rubbed with metallic wax.*

When you visit the sea, go beachcombing for small pieces of driftwood and fragments of sea-washed glass. Do not collect seashells but buy them from a reputable supplier. Some have holes already drilled for threading on to twine or raffia, but if you wish to drill holes yourself, use a small drill bit and support the shell on a lump of plastic clay. Shells can be attached to cards using glue dots. Make a tiny boat for the front of a card, using driftwood for the hull and adding a twig mast and a fabric sail.

Collect flowers and leaves and press them for future use. Many flowers also dry well. Dried roses, hydrangeas, heather and cornflowers make lovely trimmings for gift-wrapped wedding and birthday presents. Tie a sachet of dried lavender to the front of a greetings card for a delightful fragrant gift. You could even re-create a 17th-century knot garden by arranging seeds and dried lentils on areas spread with PVA (white) glue in symmetrical patterns.

These natural materials look most effective on backgrounds of handmade paper. There are some fabulous papers available incorporating petals, leaves or onion skins. If you make your own paper, making it into greetings cards is a great way to show it off. You can match the natural deckle edge of handmade paper on the other edges of a sheet by tearing it to size against a ruler. If necessary, moisten the paper first with a wet paintbrush to make it easier to tear.

## Natural materials

Use rustic fabrics such as hessian (burlap) and linen in natural, warm tones and fray the edges. Cottons woven in plaids and stripes can be cut and stuck to the front of a card in a simple patchwork design. Apply iron-on interfacing to the back of the fabrics before cutting if you wish to cut out shapes from them. Decorate the fabrics with simple embroidery stitches, keeping the colours simple or matching them to your natural decorations.

Cards and wallets can be fastened with neutral-coloured twine or string, or a few strands of undyed raffia. Make up a bouquet garni with cinnamon sticks and bay leaves and tie it on to the front of a card. Sweet-smelling sheets of beeswax are available from candle-making suppliers, and can be cut with scissors and stuck to the front of a

card with glue dots – a beehive shape accompanied by a tiny drawn bee would make a lovely design.

Recycled materials go well with natural decorations. Brown parcel paper can be stamped or painted, and wallets made from corrugated card (stock). Cut motifs from printed waxed paper cartons and attach them to cards with coloured eyelets.

Hand-deliver cards decorated with natural materials in padded envelopes for protection or put them in a box envelope.

▼ *This quick wallet of handmade paper incorporating marigold petals (right) has its side edges oversewn with dyed raffia. A pressed grass seedhead and leaf sprig decorate the front. The wallet is fastened with a raffia tie. A pretty scallop shell is the focal point of the greetings card (below left), edged on two sides with colourful handmade papers. A row of pressed forget-me-not flowerheads is applied with PVA (white) glue and a small sea-worn limpet shell is sewn to the card front with string.*

# Ethnic style

*Many nations have distinctive identities that inspire themes and styles for card making. Studying the folk art of another country is a great way to explore new craft techniques. For example, paper cuts have been a popular pastime in China, Mexico, North America, Germany and Poland for hundreds of years, and often have spiritual associations. They all have their own style and look stunning on greetings cards or adapted to make stencils.*

▲ *Characterful printed and patterned papers from all over the world can be used to make unusual and beautiful cards. This Mexican-style card (below right) has a stylized South American bird embossed on fine metal and glued to a paper coaster doiley on a bright pink card. For the Indian-inspired card (above right), scraps of printed and embroidered papers are applied in bands to the front and decorated with narrow strips of self-adhesive holographic floral designs and stickers using a paisley motif, which is a popular Indian design.*

Paper was invented by the Chinese and many of their folk crafts use it ingeniously. Traditionally, Chinese paper cuts are displayed at windows, so that the light shows through the delicate patterns. The carp, signifying wealth, is a favourite motif. Colourful Chinese paper cuts can be bought ready-made and mounted on a greetings card using spray adhesive. Chinese supermarkets sell imitation money, which can be used in découpage decorations. The Japanese also have a strong affiliation with papercrafts, with origami being the best

known. Many of the more unusual and delicate papers available today are manufactured in Japan. Thin squares of plain coloured and patterned papers for origami are widely available: use them to make origami gift boxes or assemble a collage of different patterns, which co-ordinate beautifully, to decorate a greetings card. *Washi chigiri-e* is the ancient Japanese craft of arranging torn pieces of coloured paper to make a picture, with results that can resemble watercolour or pastel. The soft washi paper can be manipulated to produce very subtle colour effects.

## National traditions

Papercrafts are very popular in Mexico, and many are incorporated in traditional festive occasions. The Aztecs made a primitive paper from bark called *amate*, and simple paper cuts of amate were thought to have magical qualities. Today, vibrantly coloured paper cuts called *papel picado* are strung up outside churches for weddings and saints' days. Try recreating traditional Mexican motifs on fine embossing metal and mounting them on brightly coloured card. Pink, lime green, orange and acid yellow are the characteristic colours of Mexican folk art. The Day of the Dead is commemorated on 31 October, when the dead are believed to return to see their loved ones. Images such as skeletons and skulls are typical features of this important festivity.

Create Indonesian batik-style designs or freehand African patterns on watercolour paper using masking fluid. Paint the paper, leave it to dry, then rub away the dried masking fluid to reveal the design and mount the picture on the front of a greetings card. Paint an Australian aboriginal design with relief paints on the top of a set of stationery.

Beautiful hand-printed and embroidered papers from India are available from specialist paper suppliers. Use them with shisha glass and bindi-style decorations on greetings cards.

Many ready-made decorations from all over the world are readily available to us nowadays. Ethnic designs are popular subjects on rubber stamps. Wood block stamps used for printing on fabric in the Far East are also available for authentic effects.

# Cards for children

*It is great fun to make cards to send to children and this is an occasion to let your imagination run wild. Go for bright colours and simple motifs. Children will especially appreciate personalized greetings, so including their name on the front of the card will make them feel special. Use a computer to write the name in a suitable font and cut it out to use as a label. Alternatively, use letter stickers or write the name using a letter stencil.*

If you are making a birthday card, add the age number, as age is very important to children and they feel very grown-up when they reach a new year. If the child has a special enthusiasm – for trains or dinosaurs, for example – create a card with that in mind. Cookie cutters are often available in the appropriate shapes, or you can find a suitable picture to use as a reference for your own template.

There are lots of novel and tactile embellishments that you can buy from craft suppliers to add to children's cards. Joggle eyes will give a comical look to a character, whether you add them to a figure you have drawn or cut out, or to a photograph. Squishy pompoms are available in different sizes and colours, and can be stuck in place with glue dots. An animal cut from felt or fleece could enclose a flat, plastic toy-making growler or squeaker, which will sound when the animal is pressed. Make sure that the felt or fleece is stuck down firmly, so prying fingers can't open it.

Small gifts can be incorporated with a child's card to make it extra interesting: you could pin a birthday badge to the front for example, or glue a few foil-wrapped chocolate coins to a Christmas tree shape to resemble baubles.

On a cautionary note, there are safety considerations to think about when making childrens' cards, and you should always bear in mind the age of the recipient. Do not decorate cards for young children with any sharp embellishments, and make sure that all decorations are stuck down securely. Use glitter paint rather than loose glitter, which could moult. If you are using brads in your design, make sure that the prongs are enclosed under a facing of card or paper, or apply stickers or tape over them, firmly stuck down.

## Child's play

Children will love to help make cards for their friends and family, and to create their own party invitations. PVA (white) glue is non-toxic, as are many water-based paints. Poster paints are an inexpensive choice for children to use, and come in bright colours that they can use straight from the pots. Cover the work surface with old plastic carrier bags cut open and laid flat to catch any spillages.

Glow-in-the-dark relief paints will make super decorations for a set of Halloween invitations. Pre-cut Neoprene shapes are available for children to stick on their cards and decorate with glitter paints, and older children love using glue and plenty of glitter to make sparkling designs. Plastic pony beads are inexpensive and are available in round, heart and star shapes. They have a large hole and are easy for little fingers to thread on to cord or thonging to make fastenings for boxes and envelopes.

▼ *This robot made of silver card (right) is trimmed with feet, hair and ears made from red sticky-backed plastic. A "door" cut in his front opens to reveal the age of the recipient. The mouth is cut out and a pair of amusing joggle eyes complete the effect. A little pair of summer sandals cut from Neoprene foam decorate a simple square card (left), which would be lovely to send to a little girl going on a trip to the seaside. The sandals are decorated with flower stickers and dots of light green glitter paint.*

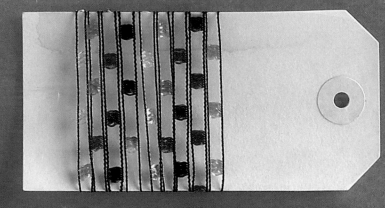

# Decorating paper and cards

This section presents masses of innovative ideas for decorating paper to use as gift wrap and to make cards and stationery. It covers background colours and ways of treating the surface of the paper, such as gilding and embossing, as well as showing the best ways to apply many different embellishments, from glitter to polymer clay motifs and pressed flowers. All the techniques described are suitable for beginners, so you can have fun mastering new crafts as well as rediscovering old ones.

# Using stencils

*Stencilling is very popular, and many ready-made stencils are suitable for adding decoration to greetings cards. Choose small-scale stencils with lots of detail, or if you like, it's quite easy to create your own stencils too.*

**1** Tape tracing paper over the design and redraw it, drawing along each side of any inner outlines to thicken them.

**2** You will need to add "bridges" between the sections to be cut out, such as on the circles on the wings of this butterfly.

**3** Transfer the stencil design on to oiled stencil board. Resting on a cutting mat, cut out the design using a craft knife.

**4** Tape the stencil to the card with masking tape. Pick up a small amount of acrylic paint with a stencil brush and dab off the excess on kitchen paper. Dab the paint through the stencil, holding the brush upright and moving it in a circular motion.

**5** Leave the first colour to dry before shading the design. Pick up a small amount of paint in a slightly different colour and apply it lightly in your chosen areas, aiming for a soft, stippled effect. Leave to dry then remove the stencil.

## STENCILLING WITH A SPONGE

For a softer, textured look, paint can also be applied through a stencil using a small natural or synthetic sponge. Don't overload the sponge with paint. Dab lightly to control the sponged effect.

◀ *This vibrant stencilled butterfly card is quick to produce once the stencil has been cut, so you could easily create a whole set of the same design, to send as party invitations for example.*

▶ *A golden cocktail glass is stencilled using a sponge and embellished with sequin dust and star-shaped sprinkles.*

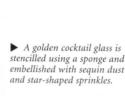

# REVERSE STENCILLING

In this alternative stencilling technique, the area surrounding the design is painted, leaving the motif the same colour as the card background. Distinctive, solid shapes work most effectively.

Draw the design on stencil card and cut out. Resting on scrap paper and working in a well-ventilated room, spray the back of the stencil with stencil mount and stick it in place. Stencil the surrounding area with a stencil brush or spray paint. Leave to dry then peel off the stencil.

▶ *An elegant dragonfly is reverse stencilled with pink spray paint on a bright yellow background, then mounted on a wavy-edged card of the same colour.*

# STENCILLING ACETATE

Stencilling paint and frosting spray on acetate gives a contemporary look to your creations. Cut stencils from sticky-backed plastic, which adheres well to the smooth surface.

I Cut a stencil from sticky-backed plastic and stick the stencil to the acetate.

2 Place the acetate on scrap paper or old newspaper. Working in a well-ventilated area, spray with paint or frosting spray.

◀ 3 Leave the paint to dry before carefully peeling off the stencil.

▲ *A stunning dress is reverse stencilled with turquoise spray paint on acetate, then embellished with stickers and silver plastic discs. The acetate is mounted on a white card trimmed with matching turquoise brads.*

# Embossing

*Three-dimensional effects can be achieved by embossing paper and thin sheet metal, working from the back of the sheet to produce a raised design on the front. The technique needs a light source, and an embossing tool. This technique offers a great way to focus attention on the interesting texture of handmade papers.*

## EMBOSSING PAPER

A stencil can be used to subtly emboss paper, and you can strengthen the design if you wish by adding a little colour to the raised area. Stencils with finely detailed outlines work best.

**1** Cut a stencil from stencil board or card (stock). Arrange the stencil on the right side of a piece of paper and secure with masking tape. Turn the paper over and rub through the stencil cut-outs with a small ball embossing tool. The embossing will be on the right side.

**2** Turn the paper over and, with the stencil still attached, highlight the embossing by rubbing metallic wax sparingly on to the motif using kitchen paper.

▲ *This coral motif is gently emphasized with a light coating of copper metallic wax, which is set off by the colour of the card and the decorative cord trimming.*

## EMBOSSING METAL

Lovely effects can be created by embossing designs on fine metal sheet, which is available from craft stores. To make the design you will need an embossing tool, which is often supplied with the metal sheet, but if you don't have a special tool, a spent ballpoint pen does the job very well. The thinner the metal sheet, the easier it is to achieve a raised effect, though very soft metal will distort easily.

**1** Tape a tracing face down on a piece of fine embossing metal. Draw over the lines with a pencil, pressing firmly to make indentations. Remove the tracing. Alternatively, lightly draw a design freehand.

**2** Place the metal right side down on two sheets of kitchen paper. Use an embossing tool or an empty ballpoint pen to redraw the design. If you wish, decorate the motif with dots or other details.

**3** Using an old pair of scissors, cut around the design just outside the embossed outline. Stick the motif in position on a card using all-purpose household glue.

# Paper Cutting

*This traditional craft skill, associated with the folk art of Europe, is a perfect technique with which to decorate gift cards, because the finished results can be designed for any size and any shape. Paper cutting requires the bare minimum of equipment, usually just a sharp pair of scissors, pencil, template and paper. Practice will make the finished outlines smooth, so choose a simple design until you've mastered the basics.*

**1** The number of times the paper is folded determines the number of cut-out images that are reproduced. A single fold creates a single image. Fold a piece of paper in half. Draw half of your pattern on the fold and cut it out. You will have a single image.

**2** Now fold a piece of paper in half and then in half again. Cut a shape out of the middle of the square, not touching any edge or fold. Open out the fold and there will be a shape cut in each section. Note that each is facing the corner of its square.

**3** For a more complex pattern, trace the pattern using a pencil. Place the tracing pencil side down, on your paper. Rub over the tracing so that the pattern is transferred. Remove the tracing paper and draw over the lines of the pattern.

**4** To start an internal cut, poke the sharp ends of the scissors into the centre of the paper that is to be removed. Then withdraw the scissors and insert the lower blade to cut out the shape.

**5** If you are using a craft knife to cut out the shape, always work with a cutting mat to protect the work surface and stop the paper slipping. Hold the knife like a pencil.

# Making polymer clay motifs

*Playing with polymer clay is a great way to try out ideas for three-dimensional motifs to decorate greetings cards. After modelling, bake the clay in a domestic oven to harden it.*

**I** Roll a piece of polymer clay to about 3mm/⅛in thick on baking parchment.

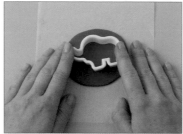

**2** Stamp the clay with a cookie cutter. Press the cutter firmly into the clay.

**3** Pull away the excess clay around the cutter. Remove the cutter.

**4** If you need a threading hole, pierce a hole in the clay with a cocktail stick (toothpick), wiggling it to enlarge the hole to take a ribbon or cord. Decorate the motif if you wish, then bake following the manufacturer's instructions. Leave to cool.

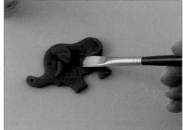

**5** Varnish the hardened motif using a specially formulated polymer clay varnish for protection if you wish. Leave to dry.

**6** Suspend the motif from the card on thread or cord or attach it with double-sided tape, adhesive foam pads or glue dots.

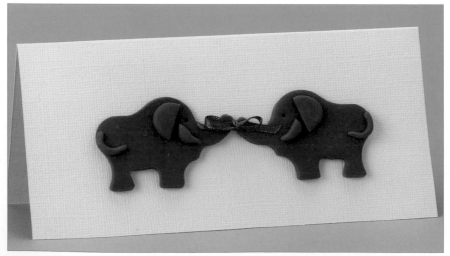

◀ *Two polymer clay elephants, joined with a bow of fine ribbon threaded through holes pierced in their trunks, are attached to the front of this card using double-sided tape.*

# USING A RUBBER STAMP ON CLAY

Rubber stamping on polymer clay produces subtle motifs that can be highlighted with metallic wax.

# MAKING A POLYMER CLAY FLOWER

Pretty clay flowers are deceptively easy to model from small balls of clay with a little simple shaping, and they have lots of decorative uses. The size of the flowers can be varied, but you need to make sure that very large motifs will not be too heavy for the front of a card.

1 Roll clay out flat on a sheet of baking parchment to about 3mm/⅛in thick and stamp firmly with a rubber stamp. Do not rock the stamp. Trim the clay around the stamped motif and bake to harden it.

1 Roll a 5mm/¼in ball of polymer clay for the flower centre and press it on to baking parchment. Roll six 5mm/¼in balls of contrasting coloured clay for the petals and press them around the flower centre.

2 Indent the flower centre at random with the head of a dressmaking pin.

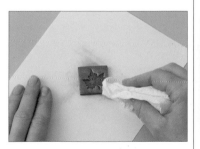

2 Resting the hardened motif on scrap paper, use kitchen paper to rub metallic wax sparingly on to the surface to distinguish the raised areas.

3 To shape the petals, indent each one close to the flower centre with the handle of a fine artist's paintbrush.

4 Bake the flowers following the manufacturer's instructions. Leave to cool then stick each flower in position on a greetings card using a glue dot.

▲ A row of delightful clay flowers are applied to a torn strip of pale green card (stock) on the front of this charming greetings card.

# Gilding

*The glimmer of fine gold, silver or copper leaf will add a touch of glamour to your handcrafted cards. Dutch metal leaf is supplied on backing paper, making it much easier to handle than real gold leaf. The effect adds a luxury element, so use this technique for cards that mark a significant occasion.*

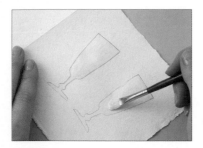

**I** Lightly draw the outline of your design in pencil on the card. Apply gold size to the shapes. Set aside for 15 minutes until the size has become clear and tacky.

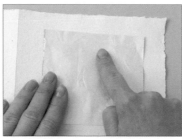

**2** Cut a piece of transfer metal leaf slightly larger than the sized area. Lay the metal leaf face down on the size and gently press in place. Peel off the backing paper.

## USING METALLIC WAX

Fabulous gilded effects can be achieved very easily by rubbing on metallic wax, which is available in a range of colours. This is a good way to add lustre to embossed papers and other raised designs: when applied sparingly, the wax will adhere just to the raised areas and highlight the embossing. Rest a small stamped motif on scrap paper, or mask a sheet of embossed paper with scrap paper or a stencil, then rub the metallic wax lightly over the motif using a piece of kitchen paper.

**3** Sweep away the excess metal leaf using a soft brush.

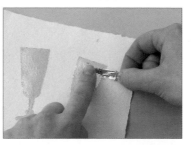

**4** If the metal leaf has not adhered in places, simply press a little of the left-over metal leaf into the gaps.

◀ *This sumptuous card decorated with a pair of gilded champagne flutes would be ideal for a special wedding greeting. The design is finished with jewellery stone bubbles and the insert is attached with a length of fine gold cord.*

# GILDING A GIFT BOX

Transform a plain cardboard box into a beautiful gilded presentation container for an important gift. Fill with shredded coloured tissue paper and tie with ribbon and beads.

1 Resting on scrap paper, use a flat paintbrush to paint the box and lid with acrylic paint. Set aside to dry.

2 Using a flat paintbrush, apply a coat of gold size to the painted box and lid. Set aside for 15 minutes until the size has become clear and feels tacky.

3 Cut a sheet of metal transfer leaf into manageable pieces. Place a piece of leaf face down on the size and gently press in place. Peel off the backing paper. Apply further sheets of metal leaf, overlapping the edges, until the box and lid are covered.

4 Sweep away the excess leaf with a soft brush. Allow the paint to show through at any gaps or at the corners of the box.

▲ *This gilded box would be lovely to use to present a gift of jewellery. For a traditional look, use light blue paint under aluminium gilding, red paint under gold gilding and aquamarine paint under copper gilding to create a verdigris effect.*

# GILDING ON POLYMER CLAY

Apply this fabulous technique to polymer clay plaques to create solid decorations. The gilding is applied before the clay is baked.

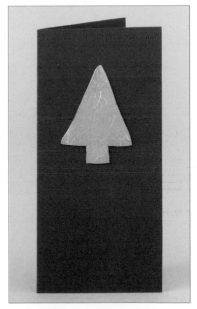

1 On a sheet of baking parchment, roll a piece of polymer clay out flat to a thickness of about 3mm/⅛in. Cut out a motif using a cutter or knife. Carefully place a piece of metal leaf face down on top of the clay.

2 Roll over the backing paper with a rolling pin. Lift off the backing paper and gently pull away any large excess pieces of the metal leaf, saving them to use again. If the gilding has not adhered in places, press a piece of the left-over metal leaf in the gaps, replace the paper and roll over it again to adhere it to the surface.

3 To create crackles in the gilding, place a piece of baking parchment on top of the motif and roll over the surface again with a rolling pin. Remove the baking parchment and bake the clay following the manufacturer's instructions.

▲ *This dramatic Christmas card has a festive tree cut from white polymer clay gilded with copper metallic leaf. The motif is applied to a midnight blue card with double-sided tape. A white paper insert allows the card to be written in clearly.*

# Creating backgrounds

*While there is a huge selection of appealing printed and patterned papers to choose from in greetings card shops, you can also make unique backgrounds using these easy printing and painting techniques.*

## PAINTING WITH A NATURAL SPONGE

Applying paint using a sponge creates a subtle, organic-looking random pattern. Use colours that harmonize well for the best effects.

**I** Using a broad, flat paintbrush, apply acrylic paint to an old plate or ceramic tile.

**2** Moisten a natural sponge. Squeeze it in kitchen paper to remove the excess water. Dab at the paint with the sponge then dab the paint at random all over the paper. Repeat with a second colour if you wish.

▲ *This orange paper has been sponged with red paint then more sparingly with off-white. The paper can be used as gift wrap or as a background for a greetings card.*

## PAINTING WITH A SYNTHETIC SPONGE

Using a synthetic sponge to apply paint gives a denser coverage of colour.

**I** Paint the top surface of a synthetic sponge with acrylic paint using a flat paintbrush.

◄ **2** Dab the sponge all over the paper. Press down on the sponge to release more paint and change the direction of the sponging to create a random effect.

▲ *Applying light pink paint at random all over cream paper using a synthetic sponge gives a simple textured effect.*

# USING MASKING FLUID

Masking fluid is used to protect areas that are to remain unpainted. After painting, the dried fluid can be rubbed away to reveal a pattern.

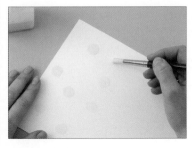

**1** Paint a simple motif or pattern with masking fluid using an artist's paintbrush on watercolour paper. Set aside to dry.

**2** Paint the paper all over with a strong colour. Leave to dry.

**3** Rub away the masking fluid patches with your finger to reveal the unpainted areas of paper underneath.

# BLEACHING

Paint freehand designs on strongly coloured papers using bleach to remove the colour from the paper. This is a super way to decorate tissue paper.

◀ Use a fine or medium artist's paintbrush to paint a simple design with household bleach. The colour should come out quickly.

▶ *Flamboyant freestyle swirls decorate this sheet of tissue paper.*

# USING CHALKS

Coloured chalks are good for creating a large patterned sheet of paper quickly. Keep the designs simple: stripes and checks work particularly well.

**1** Hold the chalk upright to draw a stripe the width of the chalk. Hold the chalk on its edge for finer lines. Draw rows of multi-coloured stripes, then add stripes in the other direction to create a check pattern.

**2** Working in a well-ventilated room and protecting the surrounding area with scrap paper, spray the chalked paper with fixative to prevent the chalk from smudging.

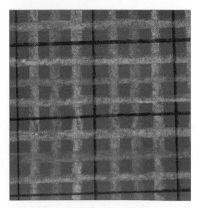

▲ *This checkered chalked paper could be used to cover a box to make a great presentation box for a baby shower present.*

# Using rubber stamps

*Applying designs with rubber stamps is a popular craft. The technique is particularly suitable for making cards, and a wide variety of styles can be created with it. Ready-made stamps are available to suit almost any theme.*

**I** Press the rubber stamp on the ink pad. If the stamp is larger than the pad, restamp it a few times to get an even coverage. Press the rubber stamp firmly on the paper or card. Do not rock the stamp. Lift off the stamp and leave the image to dry.

**2** If you wish, add a little colour to the image using felt-tipped pens.

▲ *This stamped image is mounted on a square of orange card and applied with foam adhesive pads to the card front over torn strips of green paper and floral gift wrap.*

## EMBOSSING STAMPED MOTIFS

Embossed stamped motifs have a very professional finish, which is achieved by applying embossing powder and then melting it.

**I** Resting on scrap paper, sprinkle embossing powder on the stamped image before the ink dries.

**2** Shake off the excess powder on the scrap paper. Tap the back of the image a few times to release all the excess powder. Pour the excess embossing powder back into the container.

◀ **3** Hold the stamped image over a heat source such as an electric toaster or hotplate. Alternatively, warm the image with a heat gun until the powder melts and amalgamates into a shiny, raised motif.

▲ *This regal gift tag has a feather stamped with gold ink on red card. The feather is embossed with gold embossing powder.*

# STAMPING WITH WATERCOLOUR STAMP PAINTS

Create delicate effects with watercolour paints specially formulated for rubber stamps. The paints can be blended together to produce the appearance of a hand-painted image.

**I** Paint the rubber stamp with watercolour stamp paints using a medium artist's paintbrush and blending the colours together on the stamp.

**2** Stamp the image on absorbent paper such as handmade paper or rough watercolour paper. Leave to dry.

# MAKING A FOAM STAMP

If you want a simple shape for a repeating stamped pattern it's easy to cut your own. Neoprene foam is ideal for this purpose, as you can cut it with a craft knife and it takes both ink and paint well.

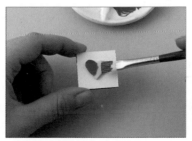

**I** Resting on a cutting mat, cut out a simple shape from Neoprene foam using a craft knife. To mount it, cut a square or rectangle of corrugated cardboard slightly larger than the foam shape. Stick the foam shape to the corrugated cardboard using all-purpose household glue.

**2** Use a flat paintbrush to paint the foam shape with acrylic paint.

**3** Stamp the image firmly on to paper or card. Repaint the foam stamp before stamping each motif.

# Adding embellishments

*All kinds of decoration can be glued on to your cards and tags to provide accents of colour and sparkle, as well as to establish a theme. The only proviso is that they should not be too heavy.*

## LOOSE GLITTER

Use loose glitter for a dense, sparkling effect on small or large areas. Pour on a generous amount to get a good even coverage: the excess can be collected and returned to the container. Glitter is widely available in a range of colours to match your designs, and can be applied to detailed shapes quite accurately if you apply the glue using a fine brush.

**1** Resting on scrap paper, spread PVA (white) glue on the area where glitter is to be applied. Depending on the size of the area, use the nozzle of the container, a glue spreader or an old paintbrush.

**2** Sprinkle glitter over the glued area and set aside to dry. Shake the excess glitter on to the scrap paper, tapping the card to remove the loose grains, and pour it back into the glitter container.

▲ *The decorated panel on this card is simple enough to work freehand with silver glitter and accent beads.*

## USING ACCENT BEADS

Use these tiny, shiny ballbearing-like beads without holes in the same way as glitter to create sparkling shapes with a crunchy texture.

**1** Resting on scrap paper, spread glue on the area to be decorated. Sprinkle the accent beads on the glue.

**2** Tap the card on the scrap paper to release the excess accent beads and carefully pour them back into the container.

## GLITTER AND BEAD SPOTS

Glitter and accent beads adhere well to glue dots, so this is a useful way to make sparkly spots of a regular size and shape.

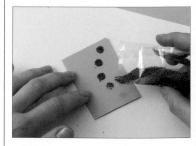

Press the glue dots on to the card surface. Resting on scrap paper, sprinkle glitter or accent beads on to the glue dots. Shake off the excess.

# USING DOUBLE-SIDED ADHESIVE SHEET

A double-sided adhesive sheet can be cut to shape and stuck to card or paper, providing a sticky surface on which to pour glitter and accent beads.

**I** Draw a motif on the paper backing of an adhesive sheet and cut it out. Peel off the backing paper and stick it in place. Peel off the protective plastic top sheet.

**2** Resting the card on scrap paper, sprinkle glitter or accent beads thickly on to the motif. Pour off the excess.

▲ *The fine particles on this demure flamingo motif catch the light beautifully. A jewellery stone eye is the only other decoration needed.*

# USING A READY-MADE ADHESIVE MOTIF

Ready-made adhesive motifs are an easy way to get a professional finish.

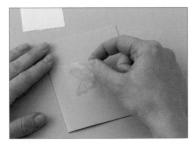  

**I** Roughly cut out the motif. Peel off the backing paper and stick the motif firmly to the card. Peel off the plastic top sheet.

**2** Resting the card on scrap paper, sprinkle glitter on the motif. Pour off the excess.

▲ *The pretty butterfly on this card is a ready-made adhesive motif that has been sprinkled with copper glitter.*

# RELIEF PAINT AND GLITTER PAINT

Both these special-effect paints can be applied straight from the container.

**I** Gently squeeze the tube to apply the paint. Leave to dry.

**2** For a glamorous effect, sprinkle sequin dust, tiny sequins or sprinkles on the paint before it dries. Gently shake off the excess.

▲ *This gift tag has wavy lines of relief and glitter paint. For extra sparkle, one line has been sprinkled with sequin dust.*

# Fabric and sewing skills

*Embroidery stitches and other sewing techniques allow you to add luxurious textures to your greetings cards and give them an unmistakably handmade look. Making too many holes in paper will weaken it, so keep your stitches large and bold, using chunky thread, string or narrow ribbon, and go for simple designs.*

## APPLYING FABRIC MOTIFS

Backing fabric with interfacing makes a flimsy fabric stiffer, and therefore makes it easier to handle when used in conjunction with paper and card (stock). It also stabilizes frail fabrics and helps prevent them from fraying excessively. The outline of the motif can be drawn on the interfacing, but bear in mind that the fabric motif will be a mirror image of the template.

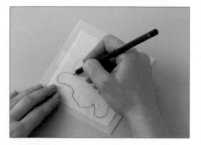

**1** Trace the outline of the motif using a black pen. Tape a piece of iron-on interfacing, shiny (adhesive) side down, on the wrong side of the tracing. Resting on a sheet of white paper so that you can see the black outline clearly, trace the motif on to the interfacing using a pencil.

**2** Roughly cut out the motif, leaving a margin all around. Position the interfacing on the wrong side of the fabric, shiny side down, and iron it on.

**3** Cut out the motif with fabric scissors and attach it to a card using spray adhesive.

▲ *A simple fabric rabbit motif has been applied to a card covered in fibrous paper. Buttons provide its bobtail and eye.*

## RUNNING STITCH

Embroidery stitches work well on paper. Holes for each end of the stitch should be pierced first so that you do not crease the surface when sewing. Do not use lightweight paper unless it has been applied to card (stock) first, as it is likely to tear. Choose threads that complement the texture and colour of the paper.

**1** Mark an even number of dots on the card for the stitches. If you prefer, mark the dots on tracing paper to use as a template. Tape the template to the card with masking tape. Resting the card on a cutting mat, pierce a hole at each dot using a bradawl.

**2** Thread a crewel embroidery needle with stranded embroidery thread (floss) and knot the end. Start the stitches on the front or back of the card: if you start stitching on the front, the end knots will be visible.

**3** Sew a running stitch in and out of the holes. Finish with a knot over the last hole and cut off the excess thread.

# LAZY DAISY STITCH

Flowers are traditional embroidery motifs, and the "lazy daisy", worked in single chain stitches, is the most familiar. It looks very pretty on a card.

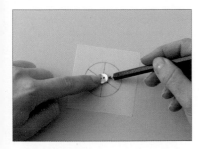

**1** To make a template, draw a circle for the flower on tracing paper. Divide the circle into six even segments. Place a button or jewellery stone at the centre and mark a dot on each segment around the centre piece. Mark another dot at the end of each spoke to mark the tips of the petals.

**2** Tape the template in position on the greetings card. Resting the card on a cutting mat, pierce a hole at each dot using a bradawl. Remove the template and glue the button or jewellery stone in position at the centre of the flower.

## BACK STITCH

This classic embroidery stitch is used to create a solid single line of stitching. Before working it on paper, pierce a row of evenly spaced holes.

Bring the needle through to the right side through the second hole, then make a backward stitch through the first hole. Bring the needle out again through the third hole and insert it in the second. Continue, taking the needle two holes forward and one back, to the end of the line.

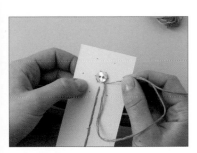

**3** Thread a crewel needle with stranded embroidery thread (floss) and knot the end. Bring the needle to the right side of the card through a hole close to the centre. Return the needle through the same hole but do not pull the thread right through.

**4** Bring the needle to the right side through the outer hole of the petal, passing it through the loop of thread. Pull the thread gently until the loop forms a rounded petal shape flat on the card.

**5** Push the needle back through the same outer hole to secure the petal. Repeat to form the other five petals, keeping the tension even throughout, and tie off the thread at the back.

▶ *An embroidered long-stemmed flower makes a lovely panel on the front of this greetings card. The button centre is applied with a glue dot. A wavy line of running stitch borders the inside of the card.*

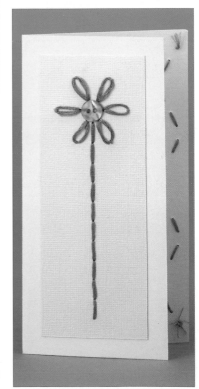

# USING RIBBON

Short scraps of ribbon can be used to embellish cards and envelopes.
Ribbon looks very effective applied in bands across the front of a card,
either singly or in multiples as stripes.

A beautiful button combined with a
scrap of lace or ribbon can be enough to
create an instant greetings card.

**1** Cut the ribbon 2cm/¾in longer than the
card front. Stick double-sided tape to
the back of the ribbon. If the ribbon is
narrower than the tape, stick the tape to a
cutting mat and cut a strip of the right
width using a craft knife and metal ruler.

**2** Peel the backing strip off the double-
sided tape. Stick the ribbon across the card
front, lining it up against a ruler to ensure
that it is straight.

**1** To attach a small button to a card,
press it on to a glue dot then lift the
dot off the backing tape. Press the
button in position.

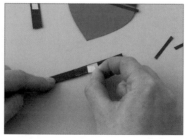

**3** Turn the card over and cut the ribbon
ends level with the card edges using a pair
of scissors.

**4** For a looser look, cut a short piece of
double-sided tape and stick it to the centre
of the ribbon only. Peel off the backing tape
and stick the ribbon in place.

**2** If you wish to sew the button to the
card, pierce holes for the stitches first.
Open the card out flat and rest it on a
cutting mat. Holding the button in
place, pierce the holes with a bradawl,
using the holes in the button as guides.

▼ *These ribbons are attached only at the
centre so that the ends hang free. The heart
motif is sewn to the card with running stitch.*

▼ *This understated card is trimmed with a
vintage button tied to a band of gingham
ribbon using stranded thread.*

▼ *The simple decoration on this small card
focuses attention on the beautiful handmade
paper with its attractive deckle edges.*

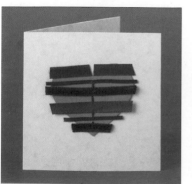

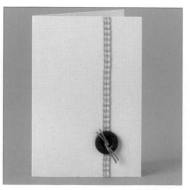

# USING BEAD EDGING

Bead edging comes in lots of designs, from simple fringing to elaborate crystal creations. Avoid heavy edging as it could make the card fall over.

I The edging is usually supplied with the beads suspended from a length of ribbon. Pull off the last few beads to the beginning of a complete sequence of beads or a single piece of fringe. Stick the ribbon end to the underside using PVA (white) glue. Repeat at the other end of the ribbon, making sure that the edging fits the card.

2 Stick a length of double-sided tape to the back of the ribbon. Peel off the backing strip and stick the ribbon in place on the card with the beads hanging down. Draw a pencil guideline or use a ruler to make sure that the ribbon is straight.

## THREADING BEADS

A vast selection of beads is available, and small individual beads of any kind can be attached to cards using thread, wire or fine ribbon or cord.

Resting the card on a cutting mat, pierce a hole at each end of each intended stitch using a bradawl. If necessary, tape a template drawn on tracing paper to the card as a guide and pierce holes through the template into the card. Sew on the beads using a running stitch or back stitch.

# USING SEQUINS

Sequins are available in a host of shapes and sizes, either loose or stitched in strips and motifs. They all make ideal card decorations.

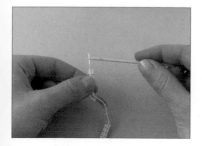

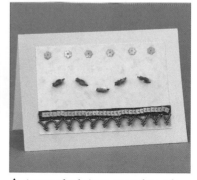

I To stop a sequin string unravelling, cut the string approximately 4cm/1½in longer than the length you need. Pull a few sequins off each end. Stick the string behind the last few sequins with PVA (white) glue, applying the glue with a cocktail stick (toothpick).

2 Stick the sequin string in place with PVA glue or all-purpose household glue, spreading the glue along the string with a cocktail stick. If necessary, line the sequins up against a ruler to get a straight line.

◀ 3 Stick loose sequins with glue dots. Press the sequin to the glue dot then lift it off the backing tape. Press the sequin on to the card. To make it easier to position a small sequin, lodge it on the tip of a craft knife blade to move it to the right place, then press down to secure.

▲ A range of techniques are used to make this pretty card decorated with beads, bead edging and sequins. The completed panel is mounted on a larger card so that the ribbon ends at the back are neatly concealed.

# The projects

Greetings cards are the perfect gesture to let someone special know that you're thinking about them. This chapter offers 55 unique and original greetings card ideas that you can make and send to family and friends to mark special occasions and seasonal events, to show that you care, as well as ideas for cards to send to help you keep in touch with friends and loved ones. Each project is illustrated with step-by-step instructions and photographs to show how it should look at every stage of making, and a list of materials required for each is included. You can copy these ideas exactly, making use of the templates provided at the back of the book, or customize them with your own colour schemes and motifs to suit the recipient and the occasion.

# New Year calendar

*This clever design emphasizes the meaning of New Year's Day as the first day of a new calendar, as you peer through the giant date to see the rest of the year cascading behind it. A shiny gold card strikes the right celebratory note.*

1 Cut off a 10cm/4in strip from one side of the gold card and reserve. Score lightly along the centre of the remaining card on the metallic side. Fold along the score line and smooth the crease using a bone folder.

2 Trace the template of the numeral 1 at the back of the book. Cut it out carefully, and centre it on the front of the card. Draw around the outline using a sharp pencil.

## materials and equipment

- craft knife
- metal ruler
- cutting mat
- 30 x 25cm/12 x 10in gold card (stock)
- bone folder
- tracing paper
- pencil
- small calendar pages
- glue stick

3 Cut out the numeral carefully using a craft knife. Use a metal ruler to get straight edges and cut the curves freehand.

4 Trim 5mm/¼in from one long and one short edge of the reserved piece of metallic card. Use the template to draw the numeral centrally on the card. Cut out the separate months from the calendar and arrange them inside the outline. When you are happy with the arrangement glue the pieces in position using a glue stick. Finally, glue the calendar card to the inside of the card front so that the calendar pages appear in the window.

# Chinese New Year

*In China red is believed to be lucky, so it is a good choice of colour to use for this pretty fan-shaped card to wish friends a happy Chinese New Year.*

1 Cut a 16 x 12cm/6¼ x 4¾in rectangle of red card using a craft knife and metal ruler. Use a bone folder to score and fold it across the centre parallel with the short edges. Trace the fan template at the back of the book and transfer the outline to the card, aligning one straight side with the fold. Cut out the fan shape using a craft knife.

2 Open the fan out flat, right side up. Using a bone folder and a ruler, score and fold across the front of the card 5mm/¼in in from the central fold to form a hinge. Refold the fan in half.

## materials and equipment

- red card (stock)
- craft knife and metal ruler
- cutting mat
- bone folder
- tracing paper
- pencil
- stencil board
- masking tape
- gold acrylic paint
- stencil brush
- kitchen paper
- single hole punch
- 30cm/12in gold cord
- embroidery scissors

3 Use the template to draw the Chinese character on stencil board. Cut out the stencil with a craft knife, resting on a cutting mat. Tape the stencil to the card front with masking tape. Pick up a small amount of gold paint with a stencil brush and dab off the excess paint on kitchen paper. Dab the paint through the stencil, holding the brush upright and moving it in a circular motion. Leave to dry, then remove the stencil.

4 Resting the card on a cutting mat, make a hole at the dot marked on the template using a single hole punch. Thread with gold cord and tie in a loop. Tie a knot 2cm/¾in from each end of the cord and fray the cord ends beyond the knots.

# Envelope Valentine

*This smart card features a tiny envelope into which you can insert a romantic message for your beloved's eyes only. The idea of mailing a love letter inspired the decorative use of lovely old stamps, franked with cherub "postmarks".*

## materials and equipment

- tracing paper and pencil
- 10 x 12cm/4 x 5in rectangle of white handmade paper
- scissors
- ruler
- bone folder
- glue stick
- 12.5 x 25cm/5 x 10in rectangle of grey Ingres paper
- old postage stamps
- cherub rubber stamp
- black ink pad
- red heart sticker

**3** Fold the Ingres paper in half to make a square card. Press the crease with a bone folder. Glue the envelope to the card, face down, then add a few vintage stamps.

**4** Finish off by printing a few cherub images across the stamps, using a black ink pad. Place your secret message in the envelope and seal the flap with a red heart sticker.

**1** Trace the envelope template from the back of the book and transfer the outline on to white handmade paper. Cut out carefully around the outside edge.

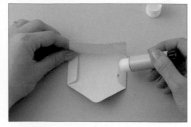

**2** Carefully score along the four marked lines. Fold in the side flaps and use a glue stick to secure them to the back flap. Fold down the triangular flap.

# Scandinavian Valentine

*This charming woven heart is a traditional Scandinavian motif. It has been given a modern twist with bold pink papers and contemporary gift wrap.*

**materials and equipment**

- brown and silver gift wrap
- pale pink card (stock)
- spray adhesive
- craft knife
- metal ruler
- cutting mat
- bone folder
- tracing paper
- pencil
- bright pink, light pink and silver paper
- glue stick
- scallop-edged scissors
- adhesive foam pads

**1** Apply brown and silver gift wrap to pale pink card using spray adhesive. Cut a 20 x 13cm/8 x 5¼in rectangle from the card using a craft knife and metal ruler and working on a cutting mat. Use a bone folder to score and fold the card across the centre, parallel with the short edges.

**2** Trace the template at the back of the book and use it to cut one heart section from bright pink paper and one from light pink paper. Cut the slits. Weave the straight ends of the heart sections together.

**3** Fold the ends of the sections to the underside of the heart and stick in place using a glue stick.

**4** Cut a 4.5cm/1¾in square of silver paper. Next cut a 5.5cm/2¼in square of bright pink paper using scallop-edged scissors. Stick the silver square on the bright pink square using spray adhesive. Stick the bright pink square to the card front with adhesive foam pads. Stick the heart to the silver square with an adhesive foam pad.

# Easter basket

*Nestle tiny Easter eggs in this charming woven basket to make a small Easter gift that will delight children and adults alike. The basket is lined with silver tissue paper and trimmed with a mesh ribbon bow on the handle.*

## materials and equipment

- light ochre and cream card (stock)
- craft knife
- metal ruler
- cutting mat
- masking tape
- bone folder
- double-sided tape
- scissors
- silver tissue paper
- 40cm/16in of 2.5cm/1in-wide wire-edged silver mesh ribbon

**1** Cut eight strips of light ochre card, each 18 × 1.5cm/7 × ⅝in, using a craft knife and metal ruler and working on a cutting mat. Arrange four strips side by side then weave the remaining four strips in and out. Adjust the strips to centre the weaving.

**2** Stick masking tape over the weaving to hold the strips in place. Score the strips along the edges of the woven section using a bone folder. Fold the extending ends of the strips upwards along the scored lines to form the basket sides.

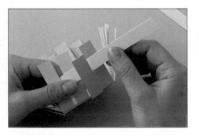

**3** Cut three strips of cream card and one of light ochre, each 29 × 1.5cm/11½ × ⅝in. Weave one cream strip in and out of the sides of the basket, folding the strip neatly at the corners.

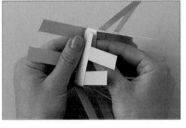

**4** Push the strip down to the base and stick in place with masking tape. Overlap the ends inside the basket and cut off the excess strip. Join the ends using double-sided tape.

**5** Weave the second cream strip then the light ochre strip in the same way, sticking the overlapped ends inside the basket with double-sided tape. Push the strips down the basket and secure with a few pieces of masking tape. Trim the extending ends level with the top of the basket using scissors.

**6** Score and fold the remaining cream strip along the centre with a bone folder. Open the strip out flat again. Stick double-sided tape to the wrong side of the strip. Stick the strip around the top of the basket on the outside, gradually peeling off the backing and matching the foldline to the top of the basket. Overlap the ends. Cut off the excess.

**7** With a pair of scissors, snip the top half of the cream strip down to the foldline at the corners of the basket. Fold the top half of the strip down inside the basket, enclosing the ends of the vertical strips. Carefully peel off the masking tape.

**8** Cut a strip of card 20 × 1.5cm/8 × ⅝in to make the handle. Stick the ends inside opposite sides of the basket using double-sided tape. Using scissors, cut two 18cm/7in squares from silver tissue paper and cut the edges in a deep zigzag. Place the tissue paper in the basket, folding under the fullness at the corners. To finish, tie wire-edged silver mesh ribbon in a bow around the handle.

# Mother's Day gift card

*This is more than just a greetings card. It's a great way to present your mum with a bracelet as a Mother's Day gift.*

## materials and equipment

- pale green card (stock)
- craft knife
- metal ruler
- cutting mat
- bone folder
- bracelet
- bradawl
- pencil
- acrylic paint
- fine artist's paintbrush
- 60cm/24in of 3mm/¹/₈in-wide satin ribbon
- embroidery scissors

**1** Cut a 21 x 14cm/8⅛ x 5½in rectangle of pale green card using a craft knife and metal ruler and working on a cutting mat. Score and fold the card across the centre, parallel with the short edges, using a bone folder.

**2** Open the card out flat on the cutting mat. Arrange the bracelet on the front of the card. Using a bradawl, pierce pairs of holes on each side of the bracelet at the top and bottom.

**3** Remove the bracelet. With a pencil, draw a small motif such as a leaf halfway between the pairs of pierced holes. Paint the motif with acrylic paint using a fine artist's paintbrush. Leave to dry.

**4** Cut two 30cm/12in lengths of ribbon and thread one length through each pair of holes. Tie each ribbon around the bracelet in a bow and trim the ends.

# Spring card with velvet chicks

*This pretty collage uses interesting materials of contrasting texture – stiff, crunchy crepe paper for the spiky grasses and soft velvet for the fluffy yellow chicks. The sky-patterned background gives the card a springlike feel.*

## materials and equipment

- double-sided olive green crepe paper
- scissors
- 10 x 15cm/4 x 6in rectangle of sky-patterned card (stock)
- glue stick
- tracing paper and pencil
- fusible bonding web
- iron and pressing cloth
- 5 x 15cm/2 x 6in strip of pale yellow velvet
- 3 black rocaille beads
- fine needle and black thread
- tiny fabric flowers

**1** Cut a 5 x 20cm/2 x 8in strip of crepe paper and snip into one edge so that it resembles blades of grass. Cut two "tufts" from one end, then attach the "grass" to the lower half of the card using a glue stick.

**2** Copy the chick template at the back of the book three times on to fusible bonding web. Iron the adhesive side to the back of the velvet and cut out the shapes.

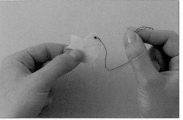

**3** Sew a black bead on to each chick to represent an eye. Iron the chicks on to the card in the spaces between the grass tufts, using a pressing cloth to protect the card.

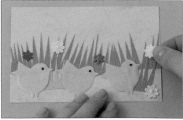

**4** Stick a few tiny fabric flowers to the grass to complete the design.

# Father's Day card

*This greetings card decorated with a handsome feather will appeal to a nature lover. The feather is protected with a piece of acetate held in place with a smart set of pewter brads, which match the elegant grey card.*

**materials and equipment**

- pewter-grey card (stock)
- craft knife
- metal ruler
- cutting mat
- bone folder
- white textured writing paper
- spray adhesive
- feather
- clear acetate
- bradawl
- 4 x 12mm/$^1$/$_2$in pewter-coloured brads

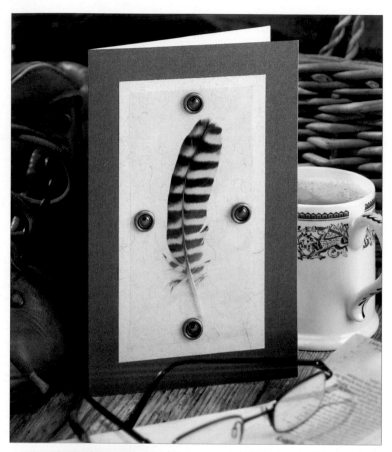

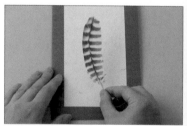

**3** Select a feather of a size that fits well on the paper panel, leaving room for the decorative brads. Spray the back of the feather with spray adhesive and stick it centrally to the paper.

**4** Cut a 15 x 7.5cm/5⅞ x 3in rectangle of clear acetate. Open the card out flat on a cutting mat. Centre the acetate rectangle on the paper panel. Pierce a hole with a bradawl through all the layers at the centre of each edge of the acetate, 8mm/⁵⁄₁₆in in from the edges. Insert a brad through each hole. Splay open the prongs inside the card.

**1** Cut a 26 x 20cm/10¼ x 8in rectangle of pewter-grey card using a craft knife and metal ruler and working on a cutting mat. Score and fold the card across the centre, parallel with the short edges, using a bone folder.

**2** Cut a 16.5 x 9cm/6½ x 3 ⅝in rectangle of white textured writing paper. Stick the paper centrally to the front of the card using spray adhesive.

**Tip**
If you wish to conceal the prongs inside the card, add a white paper insert.

# Halloween party invitation

*Invite guests to a Halloween party with this scary invitation. Visit a joke or party shop to find a selection of frightful accessories, such as this wiggly worm, to adorn the ghostly character.*

### materials and equipment

- tracing paper
- pencil
- white card (stock)
- broad black felt-tipped pen
- cutting mat
- craft knife
- plastic worm
- soft plastics glue

**I** Trace the ghost template at the back of the book and transfer it to a sheet of white card using a pencil.

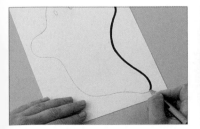

**2** Redraw the ghost outline using a broad black felt-tipped pen. Draw the eyes too.

**3** Resting on a cutting mat, cut out the ghost with a craft knife, cutting along the outer edge of the black outline.

**4** Write your message on the back of the invitation. Stick a plastic worm across the front of the card with soft plastics glue, following the manufacturer's instructions.

# Sampler for Thanksgiving

*Recreate the look of an old sampler with this appliqué Thanksgiving card. The design features a stylized tree on a fringed square of checked fabric.*

materials and equipment

- pale green card (stock)
- craft knife
- metal ruler and cutting mat
- bone folder
- 10cm/4in square of multi-coloured checked fabric
- fabric scissors
- tracing paper and pen
- iron-on interfacing
- masking tape
- sheet of white paper
- pencil
- pale green and yellow fabric
- spray adhesive
- iron
- handmade cream paper

**3** Roughly cut out the pieces, leaving a margin all round. Apply the leaves to patterned pale green fabric and the trunk to patterned yellow fabric by ironing the interfacing on to the fabric. Cut out the pieces. Stick the leaves, then the trunk, to the fabric square using spray adhesive.

**4** Tear an 11.5cm/4⅝in square of handmade cream paper, tearing the paper against a ruler. Stick the paper square to the card front then stick the fringed fabric square on top using spray adhesive.

**1** Cut a 26 × 13cm/10¼ × 5⅛in rectangle of pale green card using a craft knife and a metal ruler and working on a cutting mat. Score and fold the card across the centre, parallel with the short edges, using a bone folder. Cut a 10cm/4in square of checked fabric. Fray the edges for 5mm/¼in.

**2** Use the template at the back of the book to draw the tree and trunk on tracing paper with a black pen. Use masking tape to attach a piece of iron-on interfacing, shiny side down, to the wrong side of the tracing. Resting on a sheet of white paper so that you can see the image clearly, trace the trunk on to the interfacing. Tape a second piece of interfacing to the tracing and trace the leaves of the tree.

# Thanksgiving pumpkins

*Pumpkin pie is a traditional part of a Thanksgiving dinner, so these warmly coloured autumnal fruits make a lovely theme for a seasonal greetings card.*

## materials and equipment

- tracing paper
- pencil
- orange paper
- scissors
- textured rust brown paper
- ruler
- decorative-edged scissors
- A4 sheet of peat brown card (stock)
- bone folder
- glue stick
- 6 small skeleton leaves

**1** Trace and cut out the pumpkin template at the back of the book. Draw round it six times on the orange paper and cut out carefully around the outlines.

**2** Cut six 5cm/2in squares from the rust brown paper. Use a pair of scissors with decorative-edged blades to trim the edges of the squares.

**3** Fold the A4 card widthwise to make a long rectangle. Rub along the fold with a bone folder. Stick the rust brown squares in a checked pattern with a glue stick. Glue a pumpkin to each square.

**4** Glue a skeleton leaf in each of the spaces between the squares, making sure they all point in the same direction.

# Christmas baubles gift wrap

*Give an original treatment to an easy-to-wrap present such as a CD or book by creating a boldly coloured gift wrap on the theme of festive baubles. The bright tissue paper underneath shows the cutwork motifs to great effect. The design is easy to achieve but great accuracy is needed for a professional finish.*

**1** Wrap the present in deep yellow tissue paper. Cut a piece of bright pink paper, large enough to wrap the present in one direction and 3cm/1¼in narrower than the top of the present in the other. Trace the template at the back of the book and transfer it twice to the part of the pink paper that will lie on top of the gift.

**2** Resting the paper on a cutting mat, cut along the solid outlines of the first motif using a craft knife.

## materials and equipment

- deep yellow tissue paper
- bright pink paper
- tracing paper and pencil
- masking tape
- cutting mat and craft knife
- double-sided tape
- 2mm/¹⁄₁₆in hold punch
- tack hammer

**3** Cut away a narrow sliver of paper along the edge of the wavy string and the bauble. Cut out the other bauble in the same way.

**4** Resting the paper on a cutting mat, punch holes at random on the baubles with a 2mm/¹⁄₁₆in hole punch and tack hammer. Wrap the present, sticking the edges of the paper with double-sided tape underneath. Gently lift the cut edges of the baubles and bauble hangers so that the yellow tissue can be seen beneath them.

# Christmas landscape

*This icy winter scene is created by masking purple acetate with sticky-backed plastic then spraying it with glass-frosting spray.*

materials and equipment

- purple acetate
- cutting mat
- craft knife and metal ruler
- tracing paper and pencil
- sticky-backed plastic
- scrap paper or old newspaper
- glass frosting spray
- pinking shears
- grey card (stock)
- bone folder
- masking tape
- bradawl
- 4 x 4mm/$^5$/$_{32}$in gold brads
- white paper
- paper glue

**1** Cut an 8.5cm/3⅜in square of purple acetate. Use the template at the back of the book to cut the landscape and moon from sticky-backed plastic, working on a cutting mat. Stick the stencil to the acetate.

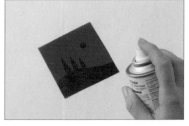

**2** Place the acetate on scrap paper or old newspaper and spray with frosting spray. Leave to dry then carefully peel off the stencil. Trim the acetate to 7.5cm/3in square using pinking shears.

**3** Cut a 21 x 19cm/8¼ x 7½in rectangle of grey card. Score and fold the card across the centre, parallel with the short edges. Open the card out flat. Cut a 5.5cm/2¼in square window on the card front, 2.5cm/1in from the top and side edges and the fold.

**4** With the open card right side up on a cutting mat, tape the acetate centrally over the window. Pierce a hole 5mm/¼in inside each corner with a bradawl. Insert a brad in each hole and remove the tape. Cut a 20 x 18cm/7¾ x 7in white paper insert. Fold the paper in half parallel with the short edges. Glue the insert inside the card, matching the folds.

# Beaded snowflake Christmas card

*This luxurious greetings card with its beautiful snowflake is easier to create than it looks. The spokes of the snowflake are made from sparkling beads threaded on to fine wire and held in place on the back of the card opening.*

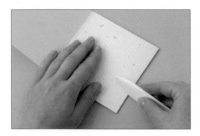

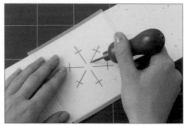

**1** Apply cream paper with metal fragments to cream card using spray adhesive. Cut a 32.5 × 11cm/12½ × 4¼in rectangle of the covered card using a craft knife and metal ruler and working on a cutting mat. On the wrong side, score the card parallel with the short edges, 11cm/4¼in from the right edge and 10.5cm/4in from the left edge. Fold along the score lines.

**2** Trace the snowflake template at the back of the book on to tracing paper using a black pen. Open the card out flat on a cutting mat, right side up. Place the template on the middle section, which will be the card front. Pierce a hole through the card at the end of the lines using a bradawl.

## materials and equipment

- cream paper with embedded metal fragments
- cream card (stock)
- spray adhesive
- craft knife
- metal ruler
- cutting mat
- bone folder
- tracing paper
- pen
- bradawl
- 70cm/28in of 0.4mm silver wire
- clear sticky tape
- 12mm/½in diameter red jewellery stone
- 72 × 3mm/⅛in red plastic beads
- wire snippers
- 5mm/¼in double-sided tape
- 6 × 6mm/¼in red square sequins
- glue dots

**3** Insert the wire in one outer hole, bend the last 2cm/¾in flat against the back of the card and tape in place. Glue the 12mm/½in diameter red stone to the centre front.

**4** Thread eight 3mm/⅛in red plastic beads on to the wire. Insert it in the hole next to the red stone and out through the hole at the opposite side of the stone.

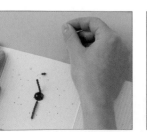

**5** Thread on eight more beads and insert the wire into the outer hole. Bring the wire to the front again through another outer hole. Repeat steps 4 and 5 to make all the spokes of the snowflake.

**6** Insert the wire through one of the remaining holes. Thread on four beads and insert the wire into the hole on the other side of the spoke. Bring the wire out through one hole beside the next spoke and repeat to make the cross pieces on all the spokes.

**7** On the back, snip the wire 2cm/¾in from the card with wire snippers. Bend the end flat against the back of the card and tape down. Fold in the card facing and stick it behind the front using double-sided tape along the edges. Stick square sequins between the spokes using glue dots.

# Christmas stocking

*This colourful felt stocking holds a present for a sweet-toothed recipient.*
*The card front is attached to the back with co-ordinating checked ribbon.*

### materials and equipment

- yellow card (stock)
- craft knife
- metal ruler
- cutting mat
- bone folder
- tracing paper
- pen
- red and green felt
- fabric scissors
- PVA (white) glue
- double hole punch
- 60cm/24in of 2.5cm/1in-wide green checked ribbon
- candy cane

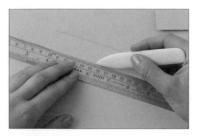

**1** Cut two rectangles of yellow card, each measuring 19 x 15cm/7½ x 6in, using a craft knife and metal ruler and working on a cutting mat. Use a bone folder to score and fold one rectangle, which will be the front of the card, 2.5cm/1in from the long left-hand edge to make a hinge. The other rectangle will be the card back.

**2** Use the template at the back of the book to cut a Christmas stocking from red felt and four spots from green felt. Stick the spots on the stocking using PVA glue.

**3** Run a line of glue along the edges of the stocking on the wrong side, leaving the upper edge free of glue. Stick the stocking on the card front, pushing the side edges slightly inwards so that the upper edge bows open. Leave to dry.

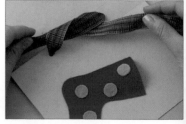

**4** Arrange the card front on the back. Punch a pair of holes centrally in the hinge using a double hole punch. Thread the ribbon through the holes and tie in a bow. Cut the ribbon ends diagonally. Slip the candy cane into the stocking. To protect the front the card will need to be hand-delivered in a padded envelope.

# Christmas reindeer

*This elegant black reindeer is created very simply, using humble flock-effect sticky-backed plastic. A diamanté collar and jewelled eye give it a touch of glamour that suits its rather haughty demeanour.*

## materials and equipment

- tracing paper
- pencil
- black flock-effect sticky-backed plastic
- craft knife
- cutting mat
- pearlized lilac card (stock)
- metal ruler
- bone folder
- 1.5cm/⅝in length of lilac and crystal diamanté trim
- glue dots
- 3mm/⅛in crystal stone sticker

**1** Trace the reindeer template at the back of the book and transfer it to the paper backing of a piece of black flock-effect sticky-backed plastic. Cut out the reindeer using a craft knife, resting on a cutting mat.

**2** Cut a 22 × 16cm/8½ × 6¼in rectangle of pearlized lilac card. Score and fold the card across the centre using a bone folder. Peel the backing paper off the reindeer.

**3** Stick the reindeer centrally on the card front. Stick a 1.5cm/⅝in length of diamanté trim to the reindeer as a collar with a glue dot at each end.

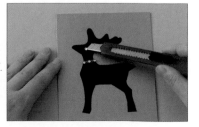

**4** To apply the crystal sticker for the eye, lift it from its backing sheet with a craft knife blade. Place in position, remove the knife then press the sticker to the reindeer.

# Baby's birthday

*Most one-year-olds will hardly notice the card you send them, but their proud parents definitely will, and any older brothers and sisters will certainly be enchanted by this fluffy bunny. And as children love to look at their collections of cards from previous birthdays, the recipient too will eventually come to treasure this one.*

**1** Cut a 24 × 15cm/9 × 6in rectangle of turquoise card using a craft knife and a metal ruler and working on a cutting mat. Score and fold the card across the centre, parallel with the short edges, using a bone folder.

**2** Use the template at the back of the book to cut the rabbit from pale pink fleece and the number 1 from yellow felt. Stick the rabbit to the front of the card using spray adhesive, positioning it 1.5cm/⅝in above the lower edge. Stick the numeral in the top left corner.

## materials and equipment

- turquoise card (stock)
- craft knife
- metal ruler
- cutting mat
- bone folder
- tracing paper
- pencil
- pale pink fleece
- yellow felt
- spray adhesive
- deep pink coloured pencil
- black relief paint
- 2cm/³⁄₄in bright pink pom-pom
- glue dot

**3** Shade the inner ears with a deep pink coloured pencil and colour the cheek to blush it. Draw the eye and nose with black relief paint. Set aside to dry.

**4** Add a bright pink pom-pom to make the rabbit's tail, attaching it with a glue dot.

# Spotty gift wrap

*Get the children to help you make this colourful gift wrap. The spots are stamped at random over the paper using simple stamps cut from thin foam. Use a range of bright paints or just one colour for a more subtle effect.*

## materials and equipment

- circle stencil
- pencil
- Neoprene foam
- cutting mat
- craft knife
- scrap of corrugated cardboard
- metal ruler
- all-purpose household glue
- flat paintbrush
- acrylic paint in red, orange and pink
- yellow paper

**1** Use a circle stencil and a pencil to draw circles measuring 3cm/1¼in, 2.5cm/1in and 2cm/¾in diameter on Neoprene foam. Resting on a cutting mat, cut out the circles using a craft knife. Cut three 3.5cm/1½in squares of corrugated cardboard. Stick each circle to a cardboard square using all-purpose household glue.

**2** With a flat paintbrush, paint one of the foam circles with red acrylic paint.

**3** Stamp the circle firmly on to yellow paper. Repeat to stamp spots at random all over the paper, repainting the foam circle each time before stamping.

**4** Clean the brush. Paint another foam circle with orange acrylic paint and stamp orange spots at random between the red ones. Clean the brush. Paint the remaining foam circle with pink acrylic paint and stamp pink spots in the gaps on the paper. Leave to dry.

# Fluttering kite card

*This breezy card is designed with a grown-up brother in mind, but no one can fail to be charmed by the little fabric kite with its flyaway tail.*

## materials and equipment

- scraps of shirting fabrics
- fabric scissors
- needle and thread
- fusible bonding web
- iron
- pencil and tracing paper
- A4 sheet of handmade paper
- bone folder
- 45cm/20in thin string
- bradawl
- glue dots
- adhesive tape
- 5 mother-of-pearl buttons
- red thread

**1** Cut out four pieces of fabric, each roughly 7.5cm/3in square, then sew them together to make a square. Trace the kite motif from the back of the book on to fusible bonding web and iron it to the back of the fabric with the crossed lines matching the seams. Cut out the kite. Fold the paper in half lengthwise and smooth the crease with a bone folder. Peel off the backing paper and iron the kite to the top right corner of the card. Draw two pencil lines for the string and the tail.

**2** From the remaining fabric cut eight 3 × 1cm/1¼ × ½in strips to make the bows on the tail. Starting 4cm/1½in from one end, knot the string over the centre of the first strip and pull the ends tightly. Do the same with the other strips, leaving regular intervals between them.

**3** Pierce holes in the card with the bradawl at both ends of the pencil tail line. Thread the string through both holes, then stick the bows down with glue dots so that the string lies along the curvy line. Cut a strip of blue fabric to go along the bottom of the card. Cut a wavy line along the top edge and fray it slightly, then attach it to the bottom edge with bonding web.

**4** Add another length of string to make the kite's string, trim the loose ends and secure on the wrong side with adhesive tape. Stitch a scattering of small buttons across the sea using red thread.

# Happy birthday cake

*For a sister who is no longer announcing her age on her birthday, make this sweet card bearing a little cake with just one candle.*

**materials and equipment**

- 12 x 15cm/5 x 6in rectangle of foam board
- craft knife
- metal ruler
- cutting mat
- 14 x 17cm/6 x 7in rectangle of striped paper
- double-sided tape
- silver paper lace
- glue stick
- 10cm/4in square of patterned wrapping paper
- tracing paper and pencil
- scraps of beige and lilac card (stock)
- white ridged paper
- pinking shears
- birthday cake candle

1 Mark an 8cm/3in square on the foam board and cut it out using a craft knife and metal ruler and working on a cutting mat. Cover the back of the striped paper with double-sided tape and remove the backing strips. Place the foam board centrally on the sticky tape and press it down firmly. Trim the surplus paper to 5mm/¼in all round and fold the edges down.

2 Cut four narrow strips of paper lace to make a frame around the opening. Stick them in place using a glue stick. Attach the wrapping paper to the back of the opening using double-sided tape, ensuring the pattern is straight and the paper lies flat.

3 Trace the cake, icing and cake paper templates at the back of the book. Cut the cake from beige card, the icing from lilac card and the cake paper from white paper. Trim the cake paper using pinking shears.

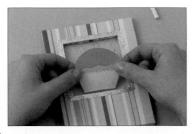

4 Assemble the three parts to make a fairy cake. Fold back the tabs and bend the cake slightly to give a three-dimensional appearance, then stick the tabs to the wrapping paper with glue dots. Glue the birthday candle behind the cake.

# Clothes closet birthday card

*Make this delightful card for a female friend who loves clothes. The panelled doors, with a little tag swinging from one handle, open to reveal a pretty print dress hanging on a little wire coat hanger.*

**1** Cut a 16 x 14.5cm/6½ x 5¾in rectangle of light pink card using a craft knife and metal ruler and working on a cutting mat. For the doors, score and fold the card 4cm/1⅝in in from, and parallel with, each short edge, using a bone folder.

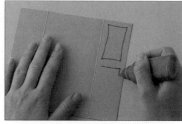

**2** Open the card out flat and draw "door panels" on the doors with bright pink relief paint. Use the template at the back of the book to cut a label from white card. Draw the number 21 on the label with the pink relief paint. Set aside to dry.

## materials and equipment

- light pink and white card (stock)
- craft knife
- metal ruler
- cutting mat
- bone folder
- bright pink relief paint
- tracing paper
- pencil
- gift wrap with small-scale floral pattern
- spray adhesive
- 20cm/8in of 8mm/⁵/₁₆in-wide deep pink ribbon
- fabric scissors
- turquoise flower sticker
- 15cm/6in of 0.8mm blue wire
- round-nosed pliers
- wire snippers
- glue dots
- 2 x 4mm/⁵/₃₂in blue square diamanté stickers
- tiny pink flower diamanté sticker
- bradawl
- 4mm/⁵/₃₂in turquoise brad

**3** Apply patterned gift wrap to a piece of white card using spray adhesive. Use the template to cut a dress from the covered card. Tie ribbon around the waist of the dress, knotting it at the front. Trim the ribbon ends diagonally. Stick a turquoise flower sticker at the neck of the dress.

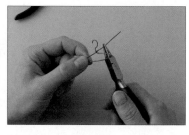

**4** Referring to the template, bend a length of thin blue wire into a coat hanger shape using round-nosed pliers. Start at the hook and finish the hanger by twisting the wire tightly around the hook. Snip off the excess wire with wire snippers.

**5** Lay the dress face down and position the hanger on top of the shoulder straps. Fold the dress tabs over the hanger and stick to the wrong side of the dress with glue dots.

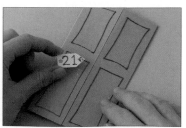

**6** Stick a blue diamanté sticker to the label at the dot and a pink flower diamanté sticker at the other end. Stick the label to the left door as if the diamanté sticker was a door knob. Stick another diamanté sticker in a matching position on the other door.

**7** Open the doors. Resting on a cutting mat, pierce a hole centrally in the card back 1.5cm/⅝in below the upper edge using a bradawl. Insert a brad through the hole. Hang the hanger on the brad. Splay open the prongs on the back of the card.

# Toolkit card

*You could send this card to a practical father (or mother, or partner) whose DIY skills you admire: it might persuade them to start on the next job.*

### materials and equipment

- 25cm/10in square of parchment-effect card (stock)
- bone folder
- 10 x 12cm/4 x 5in rectangle of parquet-effect paper
- 8 x 12cm/3 x 5in rectangle of brick-effect paper
- spray adhesive
- images of old tools from copyright-free book
- scissors
- glue stick

**I** Fold the square of parchment effect card in half and smooth along the crease with a bone folder.

**2** Stick the two pieces of decorative paper to the card front using spray adhesive and smooth down carefully.

**3** Cut out the images of the tools using scissors, following the outside edges carefully to eliminate the white background.

**4** Arrange the tool cutouts across the card and stick them down using a glue stick.

# Embroidered flowers

*This simple design is a lovely way to make use of a collection of fine patterned and handmade papers. Even small scraps in your collection can be mixed and matched to create a bouquet of pretty flowers with jewelled centres.*

### materials and equipment

- A4 sheet of card (stock)
- bone folder
- selection of patterned and plain handmade papers
- scissors
- glue stick and ruler
- tracing paper and pencil
- embroidery needle
- metallic embroidery thread (floss)
- 3 large round jewellery stones
- adhesive foam pads

**I** Fold the A4 sheet of card in half. Cut a rectangle of patterned paper to fit the front and apply it using a glue stick. Tearing against a ruler to give a deckle edge, tear a rectangle of dark handmade paper 2cm/¾in smaller all round than the card, and glue it centrally on the front.

**2** Trace the flower template from the back of the book and cut it out. Use it to cut out three plain and three patterned flowers in different papers.

**3** Thread a large-eyed needle with two strands of metallic thread. Work a round of large stitches in the centre of the three patterned flowers, to represent veins.

**4** Arrange the flowers on the handmade paper and stick them down using a glue stick. Stick jewellery stones to the patterned flower centres using adhesive foam pads.

# Greetings for a gardener

*This clever card is quick to decorate using a flower-shaped paper punch, and embossed foil makes a perfect old-fashioned watering can.*

**materials and equipment**

- tracing paper
- pencil
- 10 x 12cm/4 x 5in rectangle of craft foil
- embossing tool or blunt pencil
- ruler
- old scissors
- A4 sheet of sky-patterned card (stock)
- bone folder
- glue stick
- flower-shaped punch
- scraps of plain and patterned paper in red, purple and orange
- glue dots
- silver pen

**3** Use a flower-shaped punch to cut out at least 20 flowers from various coloured and patterned papers.

**4** Stick the flowers in place across the bottom of the card using glue dots. Using a silver pen, draw a sprinkling of water droplets spraying from the watering can.

**1** Trace the watering can template at the back of the book. Place it centrally on the wrong side of the craft foil and score around the curved parts of the outline with an embossing tool. Use a ruler as a guide to score the straight lines.

**2** Cut out the watering can using old scissors. Fold the sky-patterned card in half and rub over the crease with a bone folder. Stick the can at an angle in the top right corner of the card, using a glue stick.

# A card with a view

*This sweet picture with a nautical flavour is created from layers of torn tissue. The boat is a button, but it could also be cut out of paper or painted on card.*

## materials and equipment

- 18 x 12cm/7 x 5in rectangle of white mount board
- craft knife and metal ruler
- cutting mat
- pencil
- hole punch
- 5 eyelets and eyelet pliers
- 18 x 12cm/7 x 5in rectangle of turquoise parchment
- scraps of blue and turquoise tissue paper
- glue stick
- double-sided tape
- blue corrugated card (stock)
- button with yacht motif
- glue dots
- coloured pencil

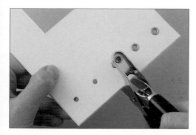

**1** Draw a 6cm/2½in square 3cm/1¼in down from the top of the mount board and centred between the side edges. Cut it out using a craft knife and metal ruler, working on a cutting mat. Mark five points evenly spaced along the lower edge of the card. Punch a hole at each point and insert an eyelet using eyelet pliers.

**2** Lightly mark the position of the square aperture on the turquoise parchment. Tear a few strips of tissue and arrange these across the lower part of the square, with the lightest colours at the back, to resemble a rough sea. Stick the tissue in place using a glue stick.

**3** Attach the parchment to the back of the board with double-sided tape, making sure the tissue paper is lined up with the square. Cut a frame from four strips of corrugated card, mitring the corners, and glue in place around the opening.

**4** Stick the button in place on the "sea" using glue dots and draw a few birds in the sky with a coloured pencil.

# Damask gift envelope

*Stencil this classic damask motif on a slim envelope designed to hold a gift token. Once you have made the stencil it is quick and easy to apply the design.*

**materials and equipment**

- jade green paper
- craft knife
- metal ruler
- cutting mat
- bone folder
- tracing paper
- pencil
- stencil board
- masking tape
- pale blue acrylic paint
- stencil brush
- kitchen paper
- 5mm/¼in-wide
  double-sided tape

**1** Referring to the techniques section, cut and fold a basic envelope 17cm/6¾in long and 8.5cm/3⅜in wide, using jade green paper. Open the envelope out flat.

**2** Use the template at the back of the book to draw the damask design on stencil board. Cut out the stencil using a craft knife, working on a cutting mat.

**3** Tape the stencil centrally to the front of the envelope. Pick up a small amount of pale blue paint with a stencil brush. Dab off the excess paint on kitchen paper. Dab the paint through the stencil, holding the brush upright and moving it in a circular motion. Leave to dry.

**4** Carefully remove the stencil to reveal the design. Apply 5mm/¼in-wide double-sided tape to the side edges of the back of the envelope, on the wrong side, between the fold and curves. Stick the back over the tabs. Apply a piece of double-sided tape to the flap to seal the envelope later.

# Embossed silver birthday card

*The texture of embossed wallpaper is a great surface to enhance with metallic wax. This card has an embossed motif highlighted with silver, on a subtle pink and grey background. Adjust the size of the card to suit your wallpaper motif.*

## materials and equipment

- grey and pale pink printed paper
- grey and pale pink card (stock)
- spray adhesive
- craft knife
- metal ruler
- cutting mat
- bone folder
- embossed wallpaper
- scrap paper
- silver metallic wax
- kitchen paper

**1** Stick the printed paper to grey card using spray adhesive. Cut a 28 x 11cm/ 11 x 5½in rectangle of the covered card using a craft knife and metal ruler. Score and fold the card across the centre, parallel with the short edges, using a bone folder.

**2** Resting on a cutting mat, cut a motif approximately 7.5cm/3in across from embossed wallpaper using a craft knife.

**3** Resting on a piece of scrap paper, rub silver metallic wax sparingly on the wallpaper motif, using kitchen paper, to highlight the raised areas.

**4** Cut a 9cm/3½in square of pale pink card. Use spray adhesive to stick the pale pink square diagonally to the front of the card then stick the wallpaper motif on top.

# Baby clothes card

*Although the arrival of a new baby means a never-ending round of washing, the sight of tiny clothes pinned to the clothes line never fails to enchant. The miniature versions on this card are equally endearing.*

**materials and equipment**

- A4 sheet of white card (stock)
- bone folder
- jade green card (stock)
- scissors
- wooden coffee stirrer
- craft knife and cutting mat
- nail file
- glue dots
- bradawl
- fine string
- 2 sticky labels
- tracing paper and pencil
- 5 mini clothes pegs (pins)
- scraps of felt
- fabric scissors
- fine white cotton
- double-sided tape

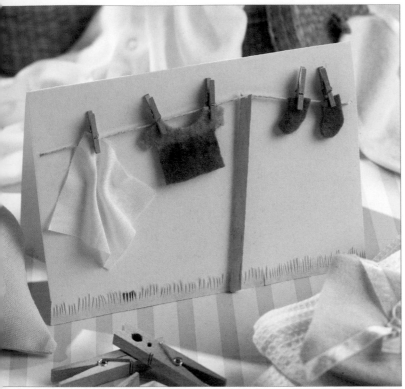

**3** Cut out a vest and sock shapes from felt and hang from the washing line with pegs.

**I** Fold the card in half parallel with the short edges and rub over the crease with a bone folder to sharpen it. Open the card out flat. Cut a narrow strip of jade card to fit along the lower edge. Snip into one edge of the jade strip to make a grass fringe, then glue in place.

**2** To make the clothes prop, cut a V-shaped notch in the end of the coffee stirrer and trim the curve from the other end. Rub it down with a nail file to smooth any rough edges. Attach it to the card with glue dots. Pierce two holes in the sides of the card with a bradawl, just under a third of the way down. Thread the string through the holes and pull taut over the prop. Cover the ends with sticky labels on the inside.

**4** Cut a 6cm (2¼in) square of fine cotton for the nappy (diaper) and peg to the line. Secure everything in place with double-sided tape and glue dots.

# Baby footprints card

*Celebrate a christening or naming day with this contemporary card of tiny stencilled footprints. The design is attached to the front of the card with star-shaped brads. Make a blue card for a boy and a pink card for a girl.*

## materials and equipment

- light blue mottled card (stock)
- craft knife
- metal ruler
- cutting mat
- bone folder
- tracing paper
- pencil
- stencil board
- white confetti paper
- masking tape
- mid-blue acrylic paint
- stencil brush
- kitchen paper
- orange polka dot paper
- spray adhesive
- bradawl
- 2 light blue 15mm/⁵/₈in star-shaped brads
- 5mm/¹/₄in-wide double-sided tape

**1** Cut a 35.5 x 17cm/14 x 6¾in rectangle of blue mottled card. On the wrong side, parallel with the short edges, score and fold the card 11.5cm/4¼in from the left edge and 12cm/4½in from the right edge.

**2** Use the template at the back of the book to cut the footprints from stencil board. Cut an 8.5 x 6cm/3⅜ x 2⅜in rectangle of white confetti paper. Tape the stencil to the paper. Pick up a little paint on the stencil brush and dab off the excess on kitchen paper. Apply the paint through the stencil, holding the brush upright and moving it in a circular motion. Leave to dry. Remove the stencil.

**3** Cut a 10 x 9cm/4 x 3½in rectangle of orange polka dot paper. Stick the stencilled panel centrally on top using spray adhesive. Open the card out. Position the panel on the card front (the middle section) and use a bradawl to pierce holes at the top and bottom of the stencilled paper.

**4** Insert the brads through the holes. Splay open the prongs inside the card. Fold the facing section inside the card front and secure the edges with double-sided tape.

# Starting school gift tag

*Here is a great gift tag to tie on a good-luck present for someone who is about to start school. The colourful pencil can be used as a bookmark.*

materials and equipment

- pen
- metal ruler
- beige laid card (stock)
- red paper
- cutting mat
- craft knife
- spray adhesive
- single hole punch
- 25cm/10in of 1cm/$^3$/$_8$in-wide blue ribbon

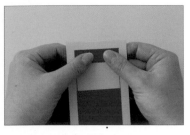

**1** Draw an 18 × 5cm/7 × 2in rectangle on beige card. From red paper, cut a 13.5 × 5cm/5¼ × 2in rectangle for the paint on the pencil and a 5 × 1.5cm/2 × ⅝in rectangle for the tip. Stick the papers on each end of the drawn rectangle using spray adhesive.

**2** Draw diagonal lines from the centre at the "tip" end of the rectangle to the corners of the "paint" to form the point of the pencil.

**3** Cut out the pencil shape using a craft knife and metal ruler and working on a cutting mat.

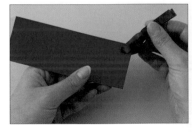

**4** Punch a hole with a single hole punch at one corner of the tag and tie a length of ribbon through the hole.

# Portfolio congratulations card

*Send a message of congratulations on an exam pass with this portfolio greetings card. The vibrant crocodile skin-effect paper is strengthened with card and the corners and spine are bound with adhesive cloth tape.*

**1** Apply crocodile skin paper to green card using spray adhesive. From the card cut two rectangles each 21 × 13cm/8¼ × 5⅛in. On the right sides draw diagonal lines across the two outer corners, beginning 5cm/2in from each corner. Stick cloth tape diagonally across the corners, along the marked lines. Trim the tape level with the straight edges.

**2** Draw a line 1cm/⅜in in from the inner long edges on both sides of both pieces of card. To make the hinge, on the right side stick a length of cloth tape to one piece of card along the marked line, with 1cm/⅜in extending at the top and bottom. Stick the other long edge of the tape to the other card, along the marked line.

## materials and equipment

- green crocodile skin-effect paper
- green card (stock)
- spray adhesive
- craft knife
- metal ruler
- cutting mat
- black pen
- 5cm/2in-wide black cloth tape
- scissors
- 50cm/20in of 2.5cm/1in-wide black grosgrain ribbon
- 2.5cm/1in-wide double-sided tape

**3** On the inside, turn in the ends of the tape and stick down. Stick a 20cm/8in length of tape to the hinge, lining up the edges with the marked lines.

**4** Cut 2.5cm/1in slits 1cm/⅜in in from the long opening edges of the portfolio. Cut the ribbon in half and thread each length through a slit. Stick the ribbon ends inside the card with double-sided tape.

# Driving test card

*Make a copy on a photocopier or computer of a photograph of a handsome old car for this card. It would be great to send to wish someone luck with their driving test or to congratulate them on passing.*

**materials and equipment**

- dark grey card (stock)
- craft knife
- metal ruler
- cutting mat
- bone folder
- translucent white paper
- single hole punch
- 2 × 8mm/⁵⁄₁₆in black eyelets
- eyelet pliers
- photocopy or reprint of photograph of old car
- 4 black photo corners

**1** Cut two 16 × 13cm/6½ × 5⅛in rectangles of grey card using a craft knife and metal ruler and working on a cutting mat. On the right side, score and fold one rectangle 2.5cm/1in from the short left edge, using a bone folder, to form the hinge. Open the rectangle out flat again. This will be the front of the card, and the other rectangle will be the back.

**2** Cut two 15.5 × 12cm/6 × 4⅝in rectangles of translucent white paper for the inserts. Assemble the card. Stack the inserts on the back, matching the short left edges. Place the front on top, with the folded edge on the left-hand side.

**3** Punch holes in the hinge 2.5cm/1in in from the upper and lower edges, using a single hole punch. Insert a black eyelet in each hole using eyelet pliers.

**4** Slip a photo corner on to each corner of the photograph. Position the photograph on the card front. Moisten the photo corners and stick in place.

# New job wallet

*Coloured acetate is fun to use and gives very effective results. Use this smart wallet to give a present or card celebrating a new job. The wallet could then be used by the recipient to hold papers or receipts.*

**1** Fold an A4 sheet of turquoise acetate in half, parallel with the short edges, and crease the fold with a bone folder. Open the acetate out flat again.

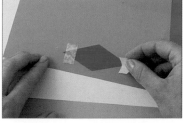

**2** Cut two 8 x 3.5cm/3⅛ x 1⅜in diamond shapes of green acetate using a craft knife and metal ruler and working on a cutting mat. Resting on a sheet of white scrap paper so that you can see the shapes clearly, tape the diamonds centrally at each end of the turquoise acetate, 5mm/¼in from the edge, on the right side.

## materials and equipment

- A4 sheet of turquoise acetate
- bone folder
- green acetate
- craft knife
- metal ruler
- cutting mat
- white scrap paper
- masking tape
- 8 chrome diamond-shaped studs
- bradawl
- 35cm/14in of silver thonging

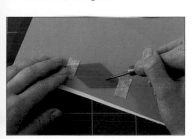

**3** Resting on scrap paper and a cutting mat, push a diamond-shaped stud into the centre of each acetate diamond. Remove the stud. Enlarge the holes made by the prongs with a bradawl. Replace the studs and push the prongs through both layers of acetate. Fold over the prongs to secure in place. Remove the masking tape.

**4** Fold the acetate in half. Resting on white scrap paper, position three studs, evenly spaced, down one side edge of the wallet. Push the prongs of the studs through the acetate and fold them over to secure. Repeat on the other side. Slip the contents inside. Fasten the wallet with thonging bound around the acetate diamonds.

# Beaded engagement card

*The fabulous colours of the gift wrap chosen to cover this card determined the bright colours of the beads used. The shiny glass and metallic beads threaded on glossy gold thread are ideal for a celebratory engagement card.*

## materials and equipment

- green and turquoise gift wrap
- deep turquoise and white card (stock)
- spray adhesive
- craft knife
- metal ruler
- cutting mat
- bone folder
- pen
- crewel embroidery needle
- gold embroidery thread (floss)
- turquoise and lime green beads
- embroidery scissors
- 5mm/¼in-wide double-sided tape

**3** Apply a total of four threads threaded with beads across the square of card, arranging them at slight angles. Knot the thread securely on the underside.

**1** Apply gift wrap to deep turquoise card using spray adhesive. Cut a 34 × 18cm/13½ × 7in rectangle of the covered card. On the wrong side, score and fold the card 11cm/4¼in from the left short edge and 11.5cm/4½in from the right short edge. Open the card out flat. Draw a 5.5cm/2⅛in square centrally on the middle section, 3cm/1¼in down from the top. Cut out the square.

**2** Cut a 7.5cm/3in square of white card. Thread a crewel embroidery needle with gold embroidery thread and knot the end. Starting 5mm/¼in in from one side edge and about 2cm/¾in from the top, bring the thread to the right side of the card square. Thread on 9–10 assorted beads. Lay the thread diagonally across the card. Push the needle back through the card, 5mm/¼in in from the opposite side edge.

**4** Apply double-sided tape around the window on the wrong side of the card. Peel off the backing strips and stick the beaded square behind the window. Fold in the facing and secure with double-sided tape.

# Vintage charm card

*Search your needlework box for pretty scraps of fabric and ribbon to make this charming wedding card. A trio of jewellery charms hang from the card front.*

## materials and equipment

- light green card (stock)
- craft knife
- metal ruler
- cutting mat
- bone folder
- scrap of vintage fabric
- pinking shears
- spray adhesive
- 3 charms
- 1 x 8mm/$^5/_{16}$in jump ring
- 10cm/4in of 5mm/$^1/_4$in-wide olive green ribbon
- fabric scissors
- glue dots

**1** Cut a 23 x 15cm/9 x 6in rectangle of light green card using a craft knife and metal ruler and working on a cutting mat. Score and fold the card across the centre, parallel with the short edges, using a bone folder.

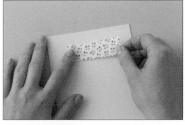

**2** Cut a 7.5 x 2.5cm/3 x 1in rectangle of fabric using pinking shears. Stick to the card front using spray adhesive, 2cm/¾in from the upper and left edges.

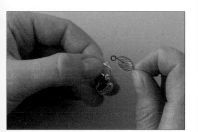

**3** Thread three charms on to a jump ring and close the ring.

**4** Tie a 10cm/4in length of 5mm/¼in-wide olive green ribbon through the ring. Cut the ends diagonally. Stick the knot of the ribbon to the fabric strip with a glue dot.

# Silver wedding gift tag

*This exquisite gift tag is sure to become a treasured memento of a special day. The number 25 is outlined with tiny jewels on acetate.*

## materials and equipment

- tracing paper
- pencil
- clear acetate
- craft knife
- metal ruler
- cutting mat
- turquoise pearlized card (stock)
- 2mm/¹/₁₆in hole punch
- tack hammer
- masking tape
- silver jewellery stone star stickers
- 25cm/10in length of silver embroidery thread (floss)

**Tip**
Instead of buying a sheet of acetate, you could use a piece of stiff clear plastic packaging to make the gift tag.

**3** Tape the acetate tag on the template. Stick jewellery stone star stickers along the outlines of the numerals, cutting between the stars on the backing paper with a craft knife. Use the craft knife to lift and position the stickers before pressing them down firmly with your finger.

**1** Trace the tag at the back of the book and use it to cut a small gift tag from clear acetate and a large gift tag from turquoise pearlized card, using a craft knife and metal ruler and working on a cutting mat.

**2** Resting both tags together on a cutting mat, punch a hole through both layers at the dot using a 2mm/¹/₁₆in hole punch and a tack hammer.

**4** Place the acetate gift tag on the card gift tag, matching the holes. Tie silver embroidery thread through the holes.

# Wedding anniversary gift trim

*This three-dimensional flower with its pearl centre and hanging loops of pearly beads is the ideal trimming for a present given for a pearl wedding anniversary, celebrated after thirty years of marriage.*

**I** Trace the flower template at the back of the book and transfer the outlines of the large and small flowers to white pearlized paper. Cut out the two flowers using a craft knife and working on a cutting mat. Overlap the end petals of each flower and stick in place with glue dots.

**2** Stick the small flower on top of the large flower, arranging the small petals between the large ones, using a glue dot at the centre. Stick a pearl bead at the centre of the flower using another glue dot.

## materials and equipment

- tracing paper
- pencil
- white pearlized paper
- craft knife
- cutting mat
- glue dots
- 8mm/⁵/₁₆in pearl bead
- 60cm/24in string of small pearl beads
- clear adhesive tape

**3** Bend a 60cm/24in string of pearl beads into three loops of different sizes. Hold the loops together at one end and bind with clear adhesive tape.

**4** Stick the bound end of the loops to a wrapped present with glue dots. Stick the flower on top with glue dots.

**Tip**
This flower trim has a timeless quality. Experiment with different paper textures, patterns and colours.

# Pearl wedding anniversary card

*Three mother-of-pearl buttons subtly mark a pearl wedding celebration on this pretty card. This is a great project for a beginner.*

## materials and equipment

- cream teardrop punched paper
- gold card (stock)
- spray adhesive
- craft knife
- metal ruler
- cutting mat
- bone folder
- pale blue patterned gift wrap
- 3 mother-of-pearl heart-shaped buttons
- glue dots

**3** Stick the torn paper to the card front using spray adhesive.

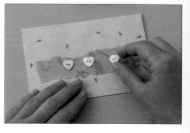

**4** Stick three mother-of-pearl heart-shaped buttons in a row to the torn paper panel using glue dots.

**1** Apply cream teardrop-punched paper to gold card with spray adhesive. (You could create your own punched paper using a hole punch.) Cut a 20 x 15cm/8 x 6in rectangle of the covered card using a craft knife and metal ruler and working on a cutting mat. Score and fold the card across the centre, parallel with the short edges, using a bone folder.

**2** Roughly tear an 11 x 3cm/4¼ x 1¼in rectangle of pale blue patterned gift wrap between your fingers.

# Ruby wedding anniversary card

*This lovely posy contains tiny flowers cut from coloured felts in shades of red, making it a great card to mark a ruby wedding anniversary.*

## materials and equipment

- pale pink card (stock)
- craft knife
- metal ruler
- cutting mat
- bone folder
- tracing paper
- pencil
- scraps of red, maroon, dark purple and green felt
- fabric scissors
- tweezers
- round and flower-shaped sequins
- glue dots
- red relief paint
- 25cm/10in of 15mm/⅝in maroon organza ribbon

**1** Cut a 17 x 10.5cm/6¾ x 4¼in rectangle of pale pink card using a craft knife and metal ruler and working on a cutting mat. Score and fold the card across the centre, parallel with the short edges, using a bone folder.

**2** Use the templates at the back of the book to cut out a total of eight flowers and circles from red, maroon and dark purple felt. Cut four leaves from green felt. Arrange the flowers and leaves in a circular group on the card front, interspersed with round and flower-shaped sequins. Use tweezers to nudge the pieces into place.

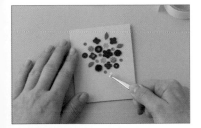

**3** Stick the flowers, leaves and sequins to the card front with glue dots. Stick small round sequins on a few of the flower centres with glue dots, using tweezers.

**4** Dot red relief paint on a few flower centres and at random around the posy. Tie the ribbon in a bow and trim the ends diagonally with scissors. Stick the bow under the posy with a glue dot.

# Golden wedding anniversary card

*Luxurious creamy handmade paper is gilded with a pair of flamboyant hearts and tied with a dramatic ribbon on this super golden wedding card.*

**materials and equipment**

- cream handmade paper
- ruler
- bone folder
- tracing paper and pencil
- flat paintbrush
- 15-minute gold size
- scissors
- sheet of gold Dutch metal transfer leaf
- soft brush
- double hole punch
- 80cm/32in of 4cm/1½in-wide gold organza ribbon
- fabric scissors

**1** Tear two 16 x 14cm/6¼ x 5½in rectangles of handmade paper by tearing the paper against a ruler.

**2** Score and fold one rectangle, which will be the front of the card, 2.5cm/1in in from the long left edge, using a bone folder, to make a hinge. The other rectangle will be the card back.

**3** Using the template at the back of the book, lightly draw two hearts at angles on the card front with a pencil. With a flat paintbrush, apply gold size to the hearts. Set aside for 15 minutes until the size has become tacky.

**4** Cut a piece of transfer gold leaf slightly larger than the pair of hearts. Lay the gold leaf face down on the hearts and gently press in place.

**5** Peel off the backing paper. Sweep away the excess gold leaf with a soft brush. If the gold leaf has not adhered in places, press a piece of the left-over leaf in the gaps.

**6** Lay the card front on the back. Punch a pair of holes centrally in the hinge using a double hole punch.

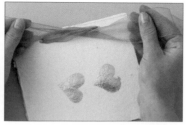

**7** Thread the ribbon through the holes and tie in a bow at the front of the hinge. Cut the ribbon ends diagonally.

# Key charm new home card

*This rustic key charm is a super motif for a new home card. The key is tied to a ready-made luggage label and hangs in front of a band of striped gift wrap.*

materials and equipment

• copper-coloured card (stock)
• craft knife
• metal ruler
• cutting mat
• bone folder
• striped gift wrap
• spray adhesive
• luggage label
• purple hemp string
• key charm
• 5mm/¹/₄in hole punch
• tack hammer
• scissors
• cream paper
• paper glue

**1** Cut a 22 × 15cm/8½ × 6in rectangle of copper card using a craft knife and metal ruler and working on a cutting mat. Score and fold the card across the centre, parallel with the short edges, using a bone folder.

**2** Cut an 11 × 6.5cm/4¼ × 2½in rectangle of striped gift wrap. Stick the gift wrap across the card front, 5cm/2in below the upper edge, using spray adhesive.

**3** Discard the string on the luggage label. Slip a length of purple hemp string through the key and the label. Open the card out flat and punch a 5mm/¼in hole centrally 1cm/⅜in below the upper edge of the front.

**4** Insert the string through the hole and knot the ends so the label and key hang in the centre of the front. Cut off the excess string. Cut a 21 × 14cm/8 × 5½in rectangle of cream paper and fold it in half. Run a line of paper glue along the fold and stick the insert inside the card, matching the folds.

# Coffee break retirement card

*This card evokes a relaxing chat between friends over mugs of coffee and would be a charming theme for a card marking a well-deserved retirement.*

**materials and equipment**

- tracing paper
- pencil
- light blue translucent paper
- broad grey felt-tipped pen
- white and blue star-printed paper
- black relief paint
- craft knife
- cutting mat
- pale orange card (stock)
- metal ruler
- bone folder
- blue and white gingham gift wrap
- spray adhesive

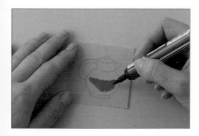

**1** Use the template at the back of the book to draw the solid lines of the percolator on light blue translucent paper with a pencil. Turn the paper over and colour the "coffee" with a grey felt-tipped pen. Leave to dry then turn the percolator to the right side.

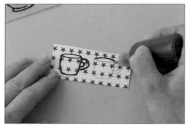

**2** Use the template to draw two mugs on white and blue star-printed paper with a pencil. Redraw the outlines of the percolator and mugs with black relief paint. Set aside to dry, then cut out the pieces, outside the black lines, using a craft knife.

**3** Cut out a 21 × 16cm/8½ × 6¼in rectangle of pale orange card (stock) using a craft knife and metal ruler and working on a cutting mat. Score and fold the card across the centre, parallel with the short edges, using a bone folder.

**4** Cut a 16 × 3cm/6¼ × 1¼in strip of gingham gift wrap. Stick the strip to the lower edge of the card front using spray adhesive. Stick the percolator and mugs to the front using spray adhesive.

# Button friendship card

*Here is a charming card to send to a friend. The colourful buttons will particularly appeal if the friend is a keen needleworker.*

## materials and equipment

- cream laid card (stock)
- craft knife
- metal ruler
- cutting mat
- bone folder
- light green handmade paper
- spray adhesive
- 4 blue, red and yellow buttons, including flower shapes
- glue dots
- bradawl
- green stranded embroidery thread (floss)
- crewel embroidery needle
- embroidery scissors
- 5mm/¹⁄₄in-wide double-sided tape

**1** Cut a 29.5 × 14cm/11¾ × 5½in rectangle of cream laid card using a craft knife and metal ruler and working on a cutting mat. On the wrong side, score and fold the card parallel with the short edges, 9.5cm/3¾in from the left edge and 10cm/4in from the right edge.

**2** Tear an 8 × 3cm/3¼ × 1¼in rectangle of green handmade paper between your fingers. Stick the torn paper to the middle section (which will be the front of the card) using spray adhesive.

**3** Arrange the buttons on the card front then stick them in place with glue dots. Open the card out flat on a cutting mat. Use a bradawl to pierce holes in the card front at the ends of the intended stems.

**4** Stitch the stems with single stitches through the pierced holes using green stranded embroidery thread and a crewel embroidery needle. Stick the facing inside the front using double-sided tape.

# Lace best wishes card

*Here is a great way to use up small scraps of pretty white edging lace in assorted designs. The lace is beautifully set off by the lovely choice of handmade and marbled papers used for the background.*

### materials and equipment

- silver marbled paper
- grey card (stock)
- spray adhesive
- craft knife
- metal ruler
- cutting mat
- bone folder
- grey handmade paper
- scraps of edging lace
- fabric scissors

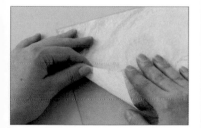

**1** Apply silver marbled paper to grey card using spray adhesive. Allow to dry. Cut a 28 x 14cm/11 x 5½in rectangle of the covered card using a craft knife and metal ruler and working on a cutting mat. Score and fold the card across the centre, parallel with the short edges, using a bone folder.

**2** Tear a 22 x 7.5cm/8⅝ x 3in rectangle of grey handmade paper by tearing the paper against a ruler. Stick the paper diagonally across the card front using spray adhesive.

**3** Turn the card over. Resting on a cutting mat, cut the excess grey paper level with the card edges using a craft knife.

**4** Stick lengths of edging lace to the grey paper using spray adhesive. Trim off the excess lace at the edges of the card using fabric scissors.

# Swedish felt motif card

*Send a "thinking of you" message with this tactile felt motif card. The angular shape of the design is inspired by traditional Swedish cross-stitch pictures.*

## materials and equipment

- red card (stock)
- craft knife and metal ruler
- cutting mat
- bone folder
- tracing paper
- black pen
- 11cm/4¼in square of iron-on interfacing
- masking tape
- pencil
- white paper
- scissors
- red and fawn felt
- iron
- spray adhesive
- pinking shears
- fawn textured paper
- paper glue

**1** Cut a 25 × 12.5cm/10 × 5in rectangle of red card using a craft knife and metal ruler and working on a cutting mat. Score and fold the card across the centre, parallel with the short edges, using a bone folder.

**2** Trace the template at the back of the book with a black pen. Tape a piece of iron-on interfacing, shiny side down, to the wrong side of the tracing using masking tape. Trace the motif on to the interfacing with a pencil, working on a sheet of white paper so that the image shows clearly.

**3** Cut out the pieces roughly, leaving a margin all round. Iron the motif on to red felt and cut out the pieces. Cut a 9.5cm/3¾in square of fawn felt with pinking shears. Stick this square to the card front then stick the motif on top using spray adhesive. Cut a 24 × 11.5cm/9½ × 4½in rectangle of fawn textured paper with pinking shears and fold it in half. Run a line of paper glue along the fold and stick the insert inside the card.

# Four-leaf clover for luck

*The meaning is clear with this simple good luck motif. The wire leaf is formed using round-nosed pliers and then sewn to the card front with fine wire.*

## materials and equipment

- white laid card (stock)
- craft knife
- metal ruler
- cutting mat
- bone folder
- round-nosed pliers
- 35cm/14in of 0.8mm green wire
- wire snippers
- bradawl
- 20cm/8in of 0.4mm green wire
- 5mm/1/4in-wide double-sided tape

**1** Cut a 28 x 13.5cm/11 x 5¼in rectangle of white laid card using a craft knife and metal ruler and working on a cutting mat. On the wrong side, score and fold the card, parallel with the short edges, 9cm/3½in from the left edge and 9.5cm/3¾in from the right edge. Open the card out flat again.

**2** With a pair of round-nosed pliers, bend the 0.8mm green wire into the four-leaf clover shape, referring to the template at the back of the book. Snip off the excess wire with wire snippers.

**3** Lay the card right side up on a cutting mat and hold the clover on the centre of the middle section (which will be the front). Pierce a hole with a bradawl on each side of the wire between the two side leaves and at each side of the end of the stem.

**4** Use 0.4mm green wire to sew the four-leaf clover to the card, bending the ends of the wire on the back to start and finish, to hold it in place. Snip off the excess wire with wire snippers. Fold in the facing section and stick it behind the front with double-sided tape along the edges.

# Starry good luck card

*The shooting stars on this glittering good luck card are attached to coloured wires bursting out of a window in the card front. A star paper punch creates the cut-outs on the lower edge. As an extra surprise, punch more stars from coloured paper to make some confetti to slip inside the card.*

## materials and equipment

- deep pink glitter card (stock)
- craft knife and metal ruler
- cutting mat
- bone folder
- 1cm/³/₈in star paper punch
- light green, yellow and turquoise pearlized card (stock)
- paper glue
- tracing paper and pencil
- 0.6mm turquoise wire
- wire snippers
- clear adhesive tape
- 5mm/¹/₄in-wide double-sided tape
- light pink paper

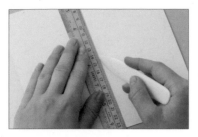

**1** Cut a 29.5 x 18cm/11¾in x 7in rectangle of deep pink glitter card using a craft knife and metal ruler and working on a cutting mat. On the wrong side, score and fold the card, parallel with the short edges, 9.5cm/3¾in from the left edge and 10cm/4in from the right edge.

**2** Open the card out flat again. Draw a 5.5cm/2¼in square on the central section, which will be the front of the card, 2.5cm/1in down from the upper edge. Cut out the square.

**3** Punch a row of five stars along the lower edge of the front using a paper punch. Make a clean cut each time, and space the stars evenly.

**4** Cut a 9.5 x 2cm/3¾ x ¾in rectangle of light green pearlized card and stick it to the wrong side of the facing (the left section) along the lower edge, using paper glue. The pearlized card should be visible through the cut-out stars.

**5** Use the template at the back of the book to cut three stars from light green, yellow and turquoise pearlized card. Snip three 9cm/3½in lengths of turquoise wire. Stick the end of each wire to the back of a star using clear adhesive tape.

**6** Stick the other ends of the three wires behind the window using clear adhesive tape. Apply double-sided tape around the window on the wrong side and peel off the backing strips.

**7** Cut a 7.5cm/3in square of light pink paper and stick the paper square behind the window.

**8** Apply double-sided tape to the outer edges of the facing. Peel off the backing strips and fold it behind the front. Punch stars in light pink paper using a paper punch to make confetti.

# Busy bee thank you card

*This charming card is also a wonderful thank you gift. The polymer clay bumble bee is held on the card with a magnet and can be removed to attach to another magnetic surface such as the refrigerator door. Adhesive magnetic sheets are available from craft suppliers and can be cut to any size.*

**materials and equipment**

- yellow, black and white polymer clay
- baking parchment
- kitchen knife
- light blue card (stock)
- craft knife
- metal ruler
- cutting mat
- bone folder
- adhesive magnetic sheet
- black felt-tipped pen

**1** Roll a 1.5cm/⅝in diameter ball of yellow polymer clay. Roll the ball into an oval to make the bee's body.

**2** On baking parchment, flatten the oval to 2cm/¾in long. Roll a 4mm/³⁄₁₆ diameter log of black polymer clay. Flatten the log to 1mm/¹⁄₂₄in thick. Lay the flattened log in two bands across the bee and cut off the excess clay using a kitchen knife.

**3** Roll a 1cm/⅜in diameter ball of white polymer clay. Cut the ball in half. Squeeze one side of the clay to a point to make a wing. Make a second wing to match, then press the wings to the top of the bee. Bake the bee following the clay manufacturer's instructions. Leave to cool.

**4** Cut a 21 × 16cm/8¼ × 6¼in rectangle of light blue card using a craft knife and metal ruler and working on a cutting mat. Score and fold the card across the centre, parallel with the short edges, using a bone folder.

**5** Cut two 1.5 × 1cm/⅝ × ⅜in pieces of adhesive magnetic sheet. Stick one piece to the underside of the bee. Stick the other piece to the card front.

**6** Place the bee on the card front. Draw a looping broken line from the bee with a black felt-tipped pen. To protect the clay bee, send the card in a padded envelope.

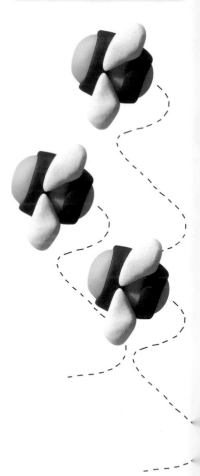

# Stencilled coral gift wrap

*Coral is believed to have healing qualities so is a good choice as a motif when giving a get well gift.*
*These jaunty branches of coral are stencilled on sea blue paper to use as gift wrap.*

## materials and equipment

- tracing paper
- pencil
- stencil board
- craft knife
- cutting mat
- light blue paper
- masking tape
- orange acrylic paint
- stencil brush
- kitchen paper

**3** Remove the stencil. Move it to a new position on the paper and tape in place.

**4** Stencil the coral again. Repeat to cover the paper. Leave to dry.

**1** Trace the coral motif template at the back of the book and transfer it to stencil board. Cut out the stencil using a craft knife, working on a cutting mat.

**2** Tape the stencil to light blue paper with masking tape. Pick up a little paint on the stencil brush and dab off the excess on kitchen paper. Holding the brush upright, apply the paint through the stencil, moving the brush in a circular motion.

# Convalescence card

*Create a restful scene of a beach hut to wish a friend a successful convalescence. The beach hut is stamped on balsa wood.*

## materials and equipment

- striped canvas effect gift wrap
- cream card (stock)
- spray adhesive
- craft knife
- metal ruler
- cutting mat
- bone folder
- 2mm/$\frac{1}{8}$in-thick balsa wood
- beach hut rubber stamp, about 5cm/2in square
- dark blue ink pad
- red paper
- all-purpose household glue

**1** Apply striped gift wrap to cream card using spray adhesive. Cut a 30 × 15cm/12 × 6in rectangle of the covered card using a craft knife and metal ruler and working on a cutting mat. Score and fold the card across the centre, parallel with the short edges, using a bone folder.

**2** Cut a 7.5 × 7cm/3 × 2¾in rectangle of balsa wood using a craft knife and metal ruler and working on a cutting mat. Press a beach hut rubber stamp on to a dark blue ink pad. Stamp the image centrally on the balsa wood rectangle. Leave to dry.

**3** Cut an 8.5 × 8cm/3½ × 3¼in rectangle of red paper and stick it centrally to the card front using spray adhesive.

**4** Stick the balsa wood panel on top using all-purpose household glue.

# Foam elephant get well card

*Amuse a sick child with this colourful card decorated with a bright blue elephant wearing a real cotton bandage around his trunk.*

**materials and equipment**

- pale green card (stock)
- craft knife
- metal ruler
- cutting mat
- bone folder
- tracing paper
- pencil
- pen
- blue Neoprene foam
- 15cm/6in of 15mm/⁵/₈in-wide white cotton tape
- fabric scissors
- all-purpose household glue
- yellow relief paint

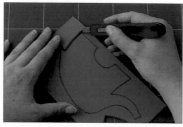

**1** Cut a 24 × 18.5cm/9½ × 7¼in rectangle of pale green card using a craft knife and metal ruler and working on a cutting mat. Score and fold the card across the centre, parallel with the short edges, using a bone folder.

**2** Trace the template at the back of the book and use it to draw the elephant and its ear on blue Neoprene foam with a pen. Cut out the pieces using a craft knife and working on a cutting mat.

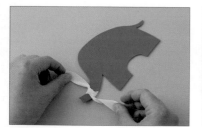

**3** Tie cotton tape in a knot around the elephant's trunk for a bandage. Trim the ends of the tape with fabric scissors.

**4** Stick the elephant to the card front using all-purpose household glue.

**5** Apply all-purpose household glue to the top of the ear on the wrong side. Stick the ear to the elephant.

**6** Dot the eye with yellow relief paint. Set aside to dry.

# Welcome home card

*Welcome a world-weary traveller home with this evocative card. Make a photocopy or a computer print-out of an old map for the background paper, and use postage stamps saved from correspondence from your friend's travels.*

## materials and equipment

- copy of an old map
- lilac card (stock)
- spray adhesive
- craft knife
- metal ruler
- cutting mat
- bone folder
- translucent purple paper
- pale grey fibrous writing paper
- 3 postage stamps
- adhesive foam pads

**1** Apply a copy of a map to card using spray adhesive. Cut a 23 × 18cm/9 × 7in rectangle of the covered card using a craft knife and metal ruler and working on a cutting mat. Score and fold the card across the centre, parallel with the short edges, using a bone folder.

**2** Cut a 13 × 5.5cm/5¼ × 2¼in rectangle of translucent purple paper and a 12 × 4.5cm/4¾ × 1¾in rectangle of pale grey fibrous writing paper. Stick the fibrous paper rectangle centrally to the purple rectangle using spray adhesive.

**3** Stick the purple rectangle to the right-hand side of the card front using spray adhesive.

**4** Stick three postage stamps in a row on the fibrous paper rectangle using adhesive foam pads.

# Letter of sympathy

*However much you want to convey your feelings to the recipient, a letter of sympathy is always difficult to compose and demands time and thought. The understated design of this paper uses a seedhead motif, with its associations with ripeness and the natural cycle – a comforting thought in the face of a sad loss.*

### materials and equipment

- seedhead rubber stamp
- yellow and orange watercolour stamp paints
- medium artist's paintbrush
- A4 handmade writing paper and envelope
- scrap paper

**1** Paint the stem on the stamp with yellow watercolour stamp paint using a medium artist's paintbrush.

**2** Blend orange and yellow paint together on the seedhead.

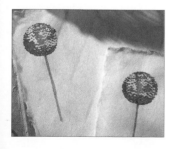

**3** Stamp the image on the writing paper. Leave to dry.

**4** Resting on scrap paper, moisten the upper edge of the writing paper. Run a line of yellow, then a thinner orange line along the moistened edge. Decorate an envelope to match. Set aside to dry.

# Bleached letterheads

*Household bleach lightens coloured papers and card and can be used to create very effective decoration for a friend when applied with a brush. This ethnic stationery with its distinctive African designs demonstrates the technique well.*

## materials and equipment

- household bleach
- non-metallic container
- fine artist's paintbrush
- brown and beige handmade writing paper and envelopes
- ruler
- spray adhesive

**1** Pour some household bleach into a non-metallic container. Dip a fine artist's paintbrush into the bleach and use it to paint the outline of a rectangle across the top of a sheet of brown handmade writing paper. Divide the rectangle into thirds with pairs of lines. The more thickly the bleach is applied, the lighter the colour will be.

**2** Using bleach, paint the outlines of two diamond shapes within each of the three sections. Paint vertical stripes in the diamonds to complete the letterhead.

**Tip**

When using household bleach, work in a ventilated area, keep away from the reach of children and wash your hands after use.

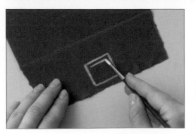

**3** Using a fine paintbrush dipped in bleach, paint the outline of a rectangle on the flap of a matching envelope. Paint a simple design within the rectangle.

**4** To decorate the beige writing paper, tear a 4.5 x 4cm/1¾ x 1½in rectangle of brown writing paper by first moistening the intended tear lines with a paintbrush then tearing along them against a ruler. Paint a design in bleach on the rectangle then stick it to the writing paper using spray adhesive.

# TEMPLATES

*Enlarge the templates on a photocopier, or trace the design and draw a grid of evenly spaced squares over your tracing. Draw a larger grid on to another piece of paper and copy the outline square by square. Draw over the lines to make sure they are continuous.*

Sampler for Thanksgiving
page 70

Chinese New Year
page 61

New Year calendar
page 60

Spring card with
velvet chicks
page 67

Halloween party invitation
page 69

Envelope Valentine
page 62

SLIT SLIT

Scandinavian Valentine
page 63

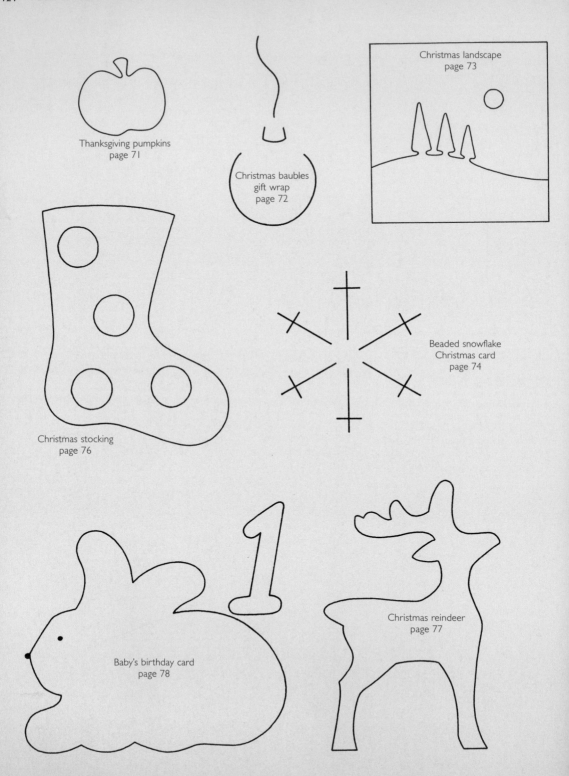

Thanksgiving pumpkins
page 71

Christmas baubles
gift wrap
page 72

Christmas landscape
page 73

Christmas stocking
page 76

Beaded snowflake
Christmas card
page 74

Baby's birthday card
page 78

Christmas reindeer
page 77

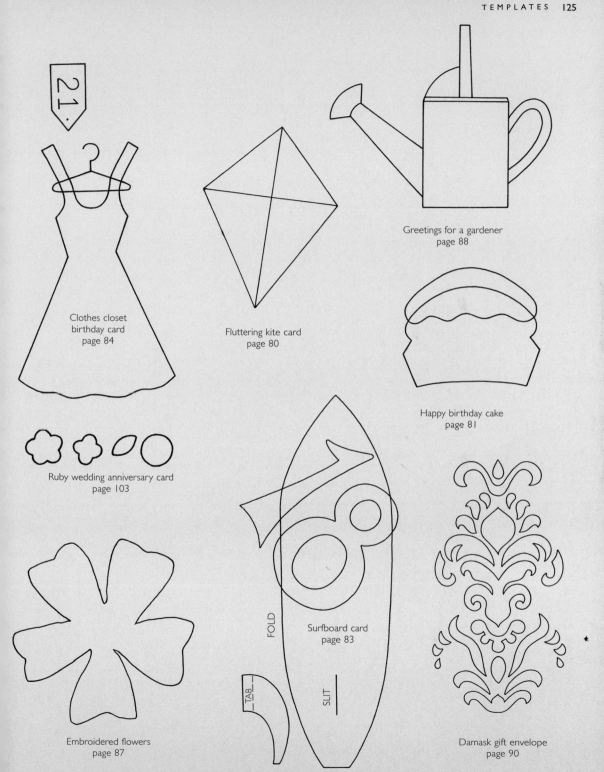

21.

Clothes closet
birthday card
page 84

Fluttering kite card
page 80

Greetings for a gardener
page 88

Happy birthday cake
page 81

Ruby wedding anniversary card
page 103

Embroidered flowers
page 87

FOLD

TAB

SLIT

Surfboard card
page 83

Damask gift envelope
page 90

Baby footprints card
page 93

Starry good luck card
page 112

Silver wedding gift tag
page 100

Four-leaf clover for luck
page 111

Wedding anniversary gift trim
page 101

Golden wedding anniversary card
page 104

Coffee break retirement card
page 107

Stencilled coral gift wrap
page 116

Swedish felt motif card
page 110

Foam elephant get well card
page 118

# INDEX